Quirky
GARDENS

Jennifer Isaacs

Quirky
GARDENS

Ten Speed Press
Berkeley, California

For my father, Geoffrey Pepperell

Ten Speed Press
P.O. Box 7123, Berkeley, CA 94707

First published 1995 by University of Queensland Press
Box 42, St Lucia, Queensland 4067 Australia.

Design by Toni Hope-Caten
Printed in Australia by McPherson's Printing Group,
Victoria
Separations by Litho Platemakers Pty Ltd, Adelaide

Cataloguing in Publication Data
on file with publisher

ISBN 0 89815 790 0

Contents

FENCES, DEFENCES AND WONDERFUL WALLS

RECYCLED MENAGERIES

TAMING NATURE

WIND AND WATER WONDERS

MINIMAL MAINTENANCE GARDENS

AUSTRALIAN LANDMARKS

AUSTRALIA, YOU'RE STANDING ON IT

Introduction

There is a long tradition in the United Kingdom and Europe of gentlemen squires dotting their estates with architectural and decorative foibles, with "follies". Fake "Gothic" castles, towers, mazes, temples and shell grottoes were built through the imagination and caprice of their owners and were not restricted by lack of wealth. Important aspects of self expression, they were usually regarded by their makers with affection, and thought of as foolish only by onlookers.

The custom of making follies in smaller cottages seems to have spread widely only in the nineteenth century. These "follettes" have their descendants in Australia where examples of domestic folk art gardens and outdoor displays of many "other" artists occur all over the country.

Australian eccentric gardens from the nineteenth and early twentieth century are now rare – the inevitable changes in land use, public park philosophy and private home ownership have removed most from the urban landscape. Yet in the late nineteenth century, it was common (even fashionable) to fill larger parks and gardens with a maze of lattice, trellis work, rough log seating and even castles and forts.

Turn-of-the-century lookouts at Katoomba and Mt Victoria in the Blue Mountains still have grotesque fake cement caves, seats and simulated tree branch structures near which visitors can rest, loiter or pose. At one time, the entire Sydney Zoo could have been described as a quirky garden menagerie of (real) animals and cement sculpture. Designed by Le Souef in the early twentieth century, cement cave enclosures of imitation rocks fashioned over chicken wire were added later by Edward Halstrom. The decorative trend spread to the suburbs. One home in Gladesville still boasts eroded cement animals from this era which startle along driveways and peer over fences.

Spectacular examples of individual domestic fantasies in shell work, mosaics and pottery collages are often local landmarks in cities throughout the world. In Mexico City, in the patio of the House of the Broken Porcelain, an interior wall fountain, ornately decorated with tiles and banquet sets of broken and unbroken seventeenth-century porcelain, imitates a fantastic basilica. Another well-known example that entraps tourists, artists and lovers of the unusual and absurd is the Grotto in Holy Ghost Park, Dickeyville, Wisconsin, built of mosaics, stones, shells and glass by Father Matthias Wernerus in 1926 when he was the parish priest.

On the outskirts of Chartres in

Lattice, forts and "Gothic" castles appeared in nineteenth century Australian public gardens and were thought sufficiently interesting to be featured on postcards.

The Millicent Shell Gardens are one of the best examples of outdoor folk art. The side fence obscures the neighbours' clothes line with distracting decorations immortalising early Australian comic characters.

France, Raymond Isidore's family compound has an internal courtyard where all facades are completely ornamented with fine glass mosaics with themes of churches, cathedrals and flowers. Most accounts of this artist's work position him as a misfit, a private maniacal ornamenter who even built a mosaic covered barn, calling it "Tombeau de l'esprit". Yet it remains a wonderful celebration of great decorative if idiosyncratic genius.

Australian examples are seldom as elaborate. The oldest decorated folk garden of porcelain pieces that survives is a small museum in Ballarat, Victoria. It dates from 1851 and was made by a Cornish woman, Caroline Warwick. This garden and that of Iris Howe in Millicent, South Australia, draw on old Celtic decorative custom of embellishing everything with shells and decorative kitchen mosaics. Such gardens were "peopled" with objects each of which speaks of its previous life. These gardens tell many stories of tea parties, family meals, cooking and social life.

An occasional gentleman's or gentlewoman's folly can be found among the grand gardens of Australia although in our egalitarian and now celebratory multicultural society, the English gentrified code of follies is abating. Far more common now are explosions of individual outlandish ingenuity in the streets of suburbia, along country back lanes, in small towns and seaside communities. Often begun on retirement, and also frequently by newer Australians, these sometimes speak of isolation and "outsiderness".

Some give vent to patriotic fervour. Others show a sense of humour in the choice of topiary subjects or arrangements of their little people (whether gnomes or lost Olympian gods). Amazing skills in harnessing wind power have produced several remarkable windmill and whirligig fantasias. Others prefer the minimalist approach. An absence of plant life and no front lawn to mow would seem to indicate a garden life of ease although the vacuum cleaner and hose might still be needed for maintenance.

The folk art gardens featuring garden foibles of the "other" artists in this book are, by their nature, ephemeral. Only four of the gardens included have been maintained beyond the life span or ownership of their makers; all others are still in the continuing process of creation. In order to survive, unusual or decorative garden spaces need to please incoming owners or be seen to have artistic or historic worth or value by the community. Castlethurso has survived within the family and several older gardens, including The Old Curiosity

Shop, Millicent Shell Gardens and Wolseley Rock Gardens, are kept up as small local tourist attractions with admission charges helping their maintenance.

Collecting these gardens together under one banner is not without linguistic problems. What are they? Folk art, local features, weird, wonderful or simply eccentric? Or should we invoke art world classifications and call them Australian examples of "outsider" art or "other" art? My old dictionary has offered me a way out of this dilemma in its definition of quirk: "a subterfuge, quibble; an individual knack or peculiarity; a clever sally, a quip". These gardens all have their quirks. They're clever, individual and occasionally subversive – quirky in fact.

They are not all "gardens" either, but are creative uses of the front and back yards. Horticulture is a secondary consideration except in the case of a few, notably the magnificent rhododendron garden of Cherry Cottage, Mt Wilson, where the blooms outshine the mosaic foibles.

The garden artists, outdoor sculptors, and artisans who made them are each expressing their own individual creativity, discovering unique techniques and forms. Most are untrammelled and unfettered by the constraints of an art history education and are making gardens, creatures, walls and decorations for appreciation by all. The galleries are their own front and back yards. With a flourish, and a great deal of hard and painstaking work, they are doing away with the conformity and anonymity of their own suburban or country street.

These gardens gently beckon, loudly call, even bellow to be noticed and admired. A few, like Arno Grotjahn's "wall of history", ask for their message to be heard as well.

The quirky gardens in this book were mostly found by word of mouth from friends, travellers and not surprisingly, a network of young artists, on whom the visual delights they offered had not been lost and who remembered their locations accurately enough for me to find them again. Ironically, considering the differing standards of good garden taste, local gardening clubs were often inadvertently helpful, as the members had certainly noticed unusual gardens in surprising detail even if they disapproved of them.

The following are extracts from a letter received in response to my queries through a local council.

...two addresses would bear your research. Unfortunately I cannot give the exact address in either case:

First: ...the property on the right hand side slopes down to the river. There are so many horrors that you could not miss it – gnomes, blackfellows, windmill, revolving orb, space shuttle, farming wheels, birds, deformities, every conceivable horror in startling contrasts black, red and white predominating...

Second: ...the front garden has a steep incline with very little garden but a few statues. The backyard has the complete "piece de resistance" collection. Every conceivable article that has been broken in the house or been washed up on the beach in the last 50 years is used with plants or "dried" arrangements in them, the most hideous contained a broken egg

beater as well as other delights. The crowning glories are the three fish ponds. One lined with black plastic, one with scarlet plastic and the other with deep blue plastic; I can assure you that the three coloured plastics absolutely dominate the scene. Arty lumps of wood,

Beau Hancock's front yard gallery displays his recycled junk sculpture, figurines, fairground fantasies and Father Christmas.

old stumps, pebbles and painted muck add to this unbelievable horror of horrors ...

Of course, appetite whetted, I resolutely set out to find these special places but succeeded in locating only one of the two mentioned – Mr Hancock's

wonderful menagerie at Dungog, New South Wales.

In the wake of post modernism, the "gardens" and sculptures of artists like Mr Hancock are being increasingly embraced into the mainstream of art practice. To some they might thereby

seem in danger of joining a "current of commonality" – but not if their makers can help it! Independent, self-motivated, irreverent and outrageously optimistic, their most frequently heard proud remark was "You won't find anything else like mine!"

Shell and Porcelain Mosaics

Shell craft was a popular Victorian pastime, particularly for young ladies who gathered at each other's homes to make scenes, floral designs and other pictures from shells they collected during seaside ramblings. These constructions were placed on the mantle along with other examples of Victorian domestic crafts: fabric flowers in glass shades, hair pictures, fretwork or perhaps oil paintings on glass.

The appeal of the seaside as a holiday venue has never abated and shell craft has continued to have sporadic bursts of popularity during the last century. Australia has numerous coastal towns in which gardeners ingeniously solved the problem of disposing of children's shell collections as well as the beautiful shells washed up at high tide and collected by the adults.

The 1930s in particular produced a revival of shell craft. Objects were made for the home or the garden: fountains were circled with clam or abalone shells, large conch or clam shells forming bird baths were mounted on pedestals as sculpture, or framed windows. Garden paths were often lined with shells, and walls and fences were given a cockle-shell stucco treatment. Only a few of these old gardens are still intact, although many artists continue to ornament fences, features and fountains with shells.

While some gardeners prefer to make mosaics exclusively of shells, others combine them with cracked porcelain and china objects which would normally be discarded – old plates, soup tureen lids, cups, teapots, handles, dolls or broken mantle ornaments. The shells used in early shell gardens around Australia reveal the changing nature of Crustacea on the Australian coast. Most were obviously obtained from eroded hillsides or were washed up by the surf. Many that appear in great profusion in gardens are now rarely found on Australian beaches. Similarly, the older porcelain mosaic gardens offer great resources of decorative domestic history – extinct patterns on tea sets, favoured motifs, what these might have meant to the community which collected them, and hints on the place they held in family life. Such gardens are eloquent if read with thought and appreciation for the messages within.

The scalloped sundial in Iris Howe's 1950s Millicent shell gardens.

A regal lion sits on his shell-encrusted throne in the magic mushroom kingdom of Millicent.

A CORNISH CURIOSITY

The oldest Australian example of Cornish decorative garden folk art is kept as a local museum called The Old Curiosity Shop in Ballarat, Victoria. The cottage and garden were made by James and Caroline Warwick, who came to Australia from Cornwall.

A small saucer and shell image from one of the mosaic house walls.

After settling in Ballarat, James Warwick earned his living as a bricklayer, making his own bricks and supplying them for many houses that were built in the town. Ballarat boomed in the gold rushes and for a period was wealthier than Melbourne itself.

The only surviving black and white photograph of the Warwicks shows them appearing like figures in a doll's house (p. 3). This old photograph is fascinating for the details it shows of the complexities of the garden developed by Caroline. Every surface, both within the garden and on the small cottage itself, has been minutely decorated with shells, coloured glass, pieces of china,

ornaments, figurines, tiles and indeed, any pretty object that seems to have caught her eye.

The garden was started in 1855 and after James' death in 1898, Caroline continued to work until her death in 1903. She seems to have been the principal decorative force at work as James was frequently away from home constructing houses or building chimneys with his bricks. Caroline ornamented the dwellings elaborately occasionally including terracotta architectural embellishments which were probably made by James. Local memories indicate that it was common for people to drop in boxes of old objects to Caroline or to

Wall decorations as they are today on the Old Curiosity Shop at Ballarat.

send their children along with anything broken from the kitchen.

In most cases the objects were placed in an organised fashion: scallop shells together to form a circular pattern; square tiles in a straight line; and broken handles from cups to form circlets. Although the teapot-edged pathway is now broken, the shards and remains of the disintegrating pottery ornaments give eloquent testimony to various aspects of internal domestic life in Ballarat in the late nineteenth century. They also reveal the importance of candles in the pre-electrical era – many circular candlestick holders feature in the designs – as do the lids of table tureens and lips of wash jugs from the bedroom.

Many people interested in decorative arts and design have taken great delight in the survival of The Old Curiosity Shop. It is now open to the public and entrance fees to both the house and garden assist in its upkeep.

MILLICENT MOSAICS

In the small town of Millicent, South Australia, one spectacular fantasy shell garden survives as a continuing source of wonder and amazement to visitors.

In 1952 Mrs Iris Howe began to construct her elaborate fairyland garden, initially for her own delight and amusement. Inspiration struck when she covered an old pair of rubber boots with shells and glass. She placed these in among the flowers in the small garden behind her cottage. Pleased with the result, she set about creating a large garden bed in the shape of a flower basket, complete with a handle. This emblematic symbol of women's culture is now a three metre

Iris Howe (aged 90) recently returned to her fantastic garden creations for the first time in 20 years.

The garden path at Millicent leads to worlds within worlds. Garden shed and tank supports are decorated with broken tile and mosaic cottage scenes topped with teapot and bottle trims. The fuchsias are inhabited and faces peer from foliage everywhere.

The views of the husband in this establishment
Are not necessarily those of the management.

First we hid the button away
The place was in a whirl
The feller that found the button first
Had to kiss the prettiest girl
I found it every time
But what a funny thing
I went home holding my trousers up
With pins and string.

Pretty maids pirouette all in a row. Mosaic detail.

flower basket completely covered with shells and mosaic patterns depicting Australian birds, parrots, a brolga, owls and robins. Mrs Howe then covered the back wall of the house using shells, mosaics and crockery to create word poem patterns, spelling out simple homilies in letters made of brown bottle glass and pieces of china.

There are four things a woman needs to know
How to look like a girl
Act like a lady
Think like a man
And work like a dog.

Don't spoil today
With tomorrow's worries
And yesterday's woes.

Man may be the head
But woman is the neck that turns it.

When singing our praise of progress in years
Try and remember the old pioneers.

Iris Howe's family and neighbours appear as circus characters on her mosaic wall.

14 *Quirky Gardens*

Mrs Howe's addiction to decoration then took hold until her entire rear garden space was embellished with highly decorative, busy shell patterns and filled with fairy tale characters, gnomes, magnificent walls of mosaics and a collection of thousands of decorative objects from bottles to kitchen crockery, each placed in a special arrangement. For Mrs Howe and indeed for many of her friends in Millicent, there was never a dilemma as to what to do with a broken piece of kitchen crockery. Mrs Howe's home became the district's recycling depot as the magnificent garden took shape. Each of the sculptural compositions was set among plantings of fuchsias, begonias, camellias, ferns, rhododendrons, cyclamen and daffodils.

Mrs Howe's original garden is probably the best Australian example of a fantasy folk art garden. In style it harks back to an older Cornish tradition somewhat like the Curiosity Shop at Ballarat, yet it also immortalises some early Australian comic characters, as well as public figures from radio and politics. Dennis the Menace, Radish, Ginger Megs, Dagwood, "Bob" Menzies, The Potts, "Waltzing Matilda", Joh Bjelke-Petersen and a poem by Jack Davey all feature.

Iris Howe's grandparents and parents came from the Millicent area, from British mining stock, "not convicts – we were disappointed to find that out". When she was nine years old, Iris's mother died in childbirth leaving her, the eldest of six children, with a great deal of domestic and emotional responsibility. Her father and uncle were skilled at plumbing and carpentry and their legacy is revealed in the technical knowledge she showed later in her garden.

At 19, Iris married Jack Howe. While their children were young the couple worked a dairy farm where she made butter which she brought to town in the "Oldsmobile utility you had to crank and crank". They moved into town in about 1939 and built their house, now know as the Shell Gardens.

Iris Howe took a dressmaking course by correspondence and when she gained her certificate, she opened a dressmaking shop on the main street of Millicent. Later she worked for the butcher, Mr Peddler, who was a relative. When someone else took over from Mr Peddler, she stopped work and, extremely bored at home, she began ornamenting the gardens.

Much of the social life of the district in the 1950s appears in the mosaic murals – one image shows the neighbours Cyril Brown (the local barber) and his wife Merle (dressed as a trick horse rider) who were card-playing friends.

Mrs Howe has lived in Adelaide since 1972 when she sold her house and garden to Don and Ailsa Salmon. Now 90 years old, Iris recently made a nostalgic trip to the garden with her daughter Jean and although her memory of the origin of some of the designs and objects has dimmed, her comments offered an insight into her obsessively resolute creativity during her Millicent years:

I can't tell you if it is an early piece or not. I used to just start something and then half way through start something else as I went along. I remember the Father Christmas and the reindeers – yes, the brainwave got me…you can make use out of everything. I bought some things – the elephant is from Adelaide. All the broken crockery from the shops would come and children's shells – people who had been to the beach would leave them for me. I would wake up in the middle of the night and have an idea in my head – daylight couldn't come quick enough.

As Mrs Howe moved around the garden, relics of her family history often prompted her thoughts.

There's Jack's old gravel spreader and I also pinched his hot water pipe from him for reinforcing. I pinched lots of things and he couldn't find them. If something was missing you'd find I'm the culprit and it's in the garden.

A section of one boundary wall – plate-faced flowers happily co-exist with the figure of an American Indian from Wild West movies.

One of the many small pixie people Iris Howe made to represent her grandchildren.

A small mosaic inscription reads "The work in this garden was done by Iris Howe, backed by Jack Howe." This causes Mrs Howe a moment of thought.

He used to say "lot of bloody rubbish, if you don't shift that I'll cart it off myself" – but it's marvellous what can be done with rubbish, with bits and pieces...

The sheer number of porcelain and cement figurines and discarded kitchen objects that this garden shelters make it a fascinating excursion into domestic history as well as a delightful example of a woman's unfettered creativity in the 1950s. The garden is one of the most important pieces of Australian folk art history.

A marvellous lengthy wall of bottles runs along one side of the property, featuring a formal arrangement of plates and topped with porcelain and glass electrical cups which are usually found on old telegraph poles. There are many vignettes that centre around the theme of a small house. Some are made in flat mosaic work on walls and others are freestanding throughout the garden – the little cottage of Snow White and the Seven Dwarfs is surrounded by its own shell garden and has shell-covered steps. Mrs Howe made one group of cement figures to represent her grand daughters.

A small grotto scene, perhaps of Iris's husband Jack Howe, musing with his pipe.

Don and Ailsa Salmon have maintained and extended the garden providing seats for visitors in their outdoor gallery.

I had a doll's head for a face mould and I did all the rest. I just worked on it with my hands and made a name for each of my grandchildren – Carolyn, Sharon, Rita, Beris, Colleen, Diane.

holes posing as either King Neptune or the Mermaid of the sea.

In the garden there are now over 115 cement figures of which Mrs Howe made 85. The present gardeners, Don and Ailsa Salmon, have continued the folk art tradition with new characters and mosaic walls. One wall which pays tribute to Australia II's win in the 1983 America's Cup includes the yacht, the winged keel, a boxing kangaroo and the Australian flag. The Salmons' art is more formal in concept with straight lines of shells and neat mosaic work. Another wall, completed for South Australia's celebrations of 150 years since the founding of the state, features the return of Halley's comet, and Sturt's desert pea, the flower emblem of South Australia.

The children who visit the garden every day, paying their donation to St John's Ambulance as they enter, are enchanted by the nursery rhyme characters who peer from the voluptuous flower beds. Snow White and the Seven Dwarfs, Humpty Dumpty, the Three Bears, the Three Pigs and the Big Bad Wolf are favourites.

The garden has been extremely well preserved by the Salmons – who have now been there almost as long as Mrs Howe was – and seating has been added for visitor comfort. Many new plantings of ornamental vegetables and double begonias have added spectacularly to its colour and horticultural content. Unlike similar gardens that have been left without a loving owner, this garden has been exceptionally well preserved and is unique in the country.

They loved to come here.

The "little people" peer and sit on every sculptured apparition, beneath mushrooms and beside huge swans. Every corner nook is conceived and managed as a space to belong to particular creatures. In one freestanding wall visitors can have their photograph taken in the manner of seaside picture postcards with their heads through the

COCKLE SHELLS ALL IN A ROW

Keith and Thelma Lowe established their shell and rock garden in 1964 in the garden beside the well-known Fryer Brothers' General Store in the Wolseley district of South Australia.

The shop, house and complex of sheds soon became host to numerous visitors who called to see the ingenious juxtaposition of shapes and objects the Lowes had created. Devonshire teas were served in the shop which also sold crafts and the garden soon brought bus loads of visitors to Wolseley. The Lowes collected shells mainly from the beaches at Robe and Kingston but many who knew about their garden also delivered bundles of shells their children had collected on seaside holidays.

Every structure in the garden (and there are many) is covered with cement stucco in which shells, stones and rocks are embedded. Most have now weathered to a soft grey. The most striking freestanding sculpture is a massive crown the interior of which is planted with flowers. In another corner stands a double storey pagoda, complete with walled gardens topped with old wrought iron sections. To one side and of unknown inspiration is the Lowes' tribute to the intrepid mariners of

Wolseley Shell and Rock Garden is fervently patriotic combining crown and country, Viking ancestors, a horse, and the roo and emu from the Aussie coat of arms.

At Wolseley, the cockle shell kanga is riveted to the spot.

ancient times, the Vikings. The place of these helmeted sea lords on the shell ship is now taken by two gnomes, one standing on the bow of the boat, the other leaning back at the rear. Their cargo in summer is a bed of bright petunias.

A large cut-out map of Australia is propped up along the side of the house; other Australian features include an upright kangaroo who stands riveted to attention by the outdoor lamp support. A backyard corrugated iron shed has a shell and rock decorated facade depicting the Australian coat of arms. Other weird and wonderful structures include shell and rock ornamented bird cages and a larger than life-size horse, possibly the Trojan Horse. The house, shop and garden was sold when Mr Lowe died and Mrs Lowe's health began to fail. For a period the shell garden fell into disrepair but it was rescued in 1993, when the current owner Dawn Davis began restoration in order to open it to the public once again.

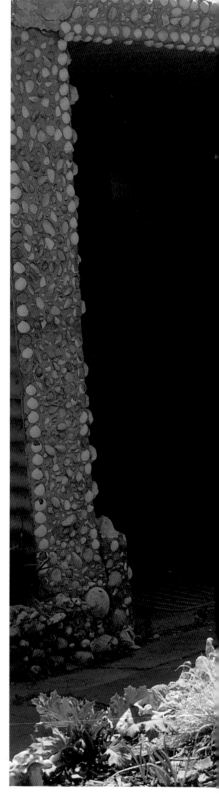

LEFT: The crumbling shell pagoda.

RIGHT: Food for thought — an Australian coat of arms in shells decorates the back yard shed behind the vegetable garden.

THE TEA GARDEN

In the fashionable Perth suburb of Mosman Park, buses bring curious visitors to see Rose Hancock's guesthouse, where Western Australia's most famous mining tycoon spent much of his time.

The tea-tree, to which all old or badly-pouring teapots are banished.

Heads peer out the bus windows, but the attention of some is captured out the other side of the bus by the front garden opposite which is a salute to the "good cuppa" by artist Evelyn Ferrier.

Evelyn's letterbox is a gutted toaster turned on its side. Surrounded by smiling bright sunflowers, it reveals its owner's incapacity to throw anything out. Indeed, all her friends and neighbours collect their broken china for her to recycle in the garden.

Behind the letterbox, the fountain appears – an array of teapots. The spouts, handles and bellies may be cracked, but nevertheless all are still capable of spurting water.

Most of the exterior walls in the back of Evelyn Ferrier's house are treated with kitchen mosaics and the inside of the house as well has not been spared.

I hate throwing things away, just because something is broken doesn't mean it is not beautiful. My place is a sort of up-market tip – people don't know what to do with their treasures, so they bring them to me – I even find boxes of china on my front door step that I don't know where they've come from. Every piece has its own story.

The "tea tree" out the back began when Evelyn was clearing out the house for a party. She had accumulated quite a few teapots, at least 20, so decided to ornament a tree near her mosaic wall.

They've bloomed happily there ever since. I have plans to grow a family tree (people), a palmistry (hands and limbs), some gentry (male characters) and a country (numbers).

Trained as a sculptor at Claremont School of Art, Evelyn used her creativity designing, making and embellishing decorative wedding and ball gowns while bringing up four children. Housebound, she then turned her attention to the walls and garden. Her home became a haven and a playground, not only for the children but also for herself.

My home is my playpen, I just love it, I don't worry about the effect on the house value – a real estate agent told me it wouldn't matter at all, just reduce the numbers interested! – but I find more are interested to judge from the people who stop.

The teapot fountain where a tea pouring ceremony is in perpetual motion.

Gentlemen's Follies

The "Portuguese Wall" on the Cherry Cottage estate at Mount Wilson, New South Wales.

Gentlemen's follies seem to date from the eighteenth century when every English estate had extraordinary towers, pagodas and grottoes. In the nineteenth century fake "Gothic" castles were built and shells began to be used as decorative features on cottages as well as in the grottoes of the wealthy.

Outlandish ornamental features have long been acceptable among the manicured lawns and vistas of English country gentlemen. Indeed, the exhibition of some degree of eccentricity could be said to be a mark of membership of the aristocracy. Most of these gardens indicate a certain contrary nature – a trick on the viewer, or a pun by the owner. One of the most unusual is Faringdon House in Oxfordshire which once boasted flocks of dyed doves, urns dripping with plastic greenery and a remarkable series of castellated structures set throughout the grounds. The most notorious of these was called "The Folly" – a 44 metre brick garden tower with a single room at the top overlooking the surrounding countryside. The room was meant to house only a grand piano, but in the end the owner could not get the piano up there. Today this folly is an accepted part of the local landscape and the subject of much amused comment.

There are garden estates in Australia which perhaps play on the implicit historical right of a gentleman (or gentlewoman) to express eccentric features of wayward aestheticism on his or her own estate. Conformity is indeed for the masses.

Garden features that suit the folly mode include hidden garden seats, walks, quiet nooks for contemplation and other unusual elements of unreality or surprise in statuary or sculptures. The gardens themselves are often spectacular in their own right, demonstrating a remarkable knowledge of horticulture (and usually requiring a large budget) to provide a sense of space and beauty for their residents.

CHERRY COTTAGE

People go to Mount Wilson because of the gardens. They live there, buy houses, or visit in spring because of a serious interest in gardens in the grand tradition of Sir Edwin Lutyens, Vita Sackville-West and Gertrude Jekyll.

These names come easily to the lips of the locals as they discuss the petal formations of the latest hybrid rhododendrons. No one ever calls for a cup of tea without bringing a plant, or a cutting, as the subject of discussion for the day.

In spring the cherries bloom and rhododendrons burst into colour beneath the tallest conifers in the mountains. This small pocket of rainforest has one of the highest rainfalls of the Blue Mountain communities and spectacular trees have grown in its dank and fertile soil throughout the centuries.

Amidst the beautiful gardens is one special place, Cherry Cottage, the creation of two brothers, Jim and Richard Prentice. The eight acre garden was created by the brothers over 30 years. The "follies" throughout the acreage are Jim's alone: all built constructions (mainly seats, gates and walls of various designs), some are ornately decorated with naive ceramic and stone mosaics reminiscent of Portuguese or Persian decorative arts. To make the panels Jim assembled a frame of dahlia stakes and laid coloured stones face down in a pattern. Over this he patted in cement, then bird wire, then

Jim Prentice's first folly, sometimes called "Not Ned Kelly", demands attention among the cherubs favoured by his brother Richard.

Cherubs representing the four seasons greet strollers along the cherry blossom walk.

more cement. When it was set the patterned tiles and stones were cleaned of grit and cement with a wire brush. Like a bower bird, Jim visited many suppliers of ornamental stones, tiles and pebbles, as well as obtaining bauxite from Lightning Ridge, and white pebbles from Cowra to form his palette. Each construction or sculpture is given a name: for instance the Persian Seat, the Moon Gate, Just a Feature, Pleasance and Park Plinth.

In all there are at least five gates at Cherry Cottage. The first, as you walk up the driveway past the stone and tile effigy of Cherry Cottage that stands as a letterbox, is a formal and quite beautifully constructed entrance gate of stacked flat stones. Within the garden are

Jim Prentice designed and constructed the "follies" of Cherry Cottage over the past 20 years.

more: the Moon Gate – a beautiful circular archway frames a July-flowering weeping apricot; the metal Clover Gate which leads from Jim's area to Richard's open meadow of daffodils; the Butterfly Gate which leads off the drive or mollis azalea walk; and the Pleasance Gate, in an incomplete fragmented wall now covered with flowering white clematis, built as a spectacular homage to the old Pleasance Courtyard in the Sydney University Union.

Approaching Cherry Cottage through the front gate, the cherry walk is before you. The light they let through dapples on the multitude of flowering bulbs that edge the path and gradually we are

introduced to pairs of cherubs representing The Four Seasons.

The first of Jim's follies to appear is perhaps his most successful in classical design terms – a black and white cement and pebble tribute to the garden seats designed by Edwin Lutyens so beloved by Gertrude Jekyll. Proceeding further up the long birch drive, lulled by the bees, the hazy Blue Mountain light and the pink and blue flowers, one is soon startled as the first of the unusual sculptures rears up. In Jim's design notes it is called "Not Ned Kelly" but it is now known as the Beehive. The dark sculpture leans at an angle reminiscent of Bathurst Island pukumani poles and is a sign that more

unusual pleasures are in store.

Low stone walls capped with Jim Prentice's handmade pebble mosaic tiles lead to seats and gates in many nooks. One, for contemplation and quiet thought, is the Spinney, where a shrine to the owners' mother is tended. Another is completely hidden, hence its name: Garden Secrets – "This place is so secret even the owners don't go there," Jim Prentice remarked. Lily-of-the-valley carpets the ground before a heavy seat structure that is rather like a throne for three.

The largest of the simple stone structures is the Moon Gate which frames an elegant lawn, complete with a sundial which Jim carved out of a square of dimension stone. Unlike the other follies which were transported in sections from Sydney, it was made on site over a framework of steel rods to take the weight. The flat basalt stones used in its construction were gathered at Mt Tomah and transported to the garden.

Cherry Cottage was originally the caretaker's cottage of a larger pioneer Mt Wilson estate, Yengo. The land was crisscrossed with hawthorn hedges enclosing the orchard and horses. Yengo was subdivided in 1964 when the Prentice brothers purchased the cottage and 8 acres.

It was a job and a half to clear the land. We ripped out the hawthorn hedges and replaced them with plants. The big old trees were there, but we planted everything else. The soil had been flogged. There was no humus in it and the water was not on for some time.

Each brother has a house on the property. Jim has lived full time in the caretaker's cottage (a soft lavender-blue painted timber dwelling completed in 1880 at the same time as Yengo) since his retirement from a lifelong career in the Westpac bank. When Richard retired from university administration in 1984 he built an imposing double-storey red brick residence surrounded with new plantings of azaleas, daffodils, cherry trees and red rhododendrons. His is a bright and aggressive flash of colour in the rainforest whereas Jim's taste is more subdued, the blues, whites and pinks.

The garden is now well known and featured in the Blue Mountains Open Garden Festival each year when

ABOVE: The Pleasance, a non-opening folly of a gate set in an unfinished stone and mosaic wall – now a beautiful clematis-covered ruin.

BELOW: A close view of the Portuguese Wall mosaics reveals a homage to Westpac Bank where Jim Prentice worked until his retirement.

numerous visitors appear up the long drive to look in wonder at the groves and bays of the garden. Cherry Cottage contains one of the finest collections of cool climate plants in Australia.

Many visitors have heard of Jim's follies although Richard consoles himself, probably accurately, that more are visiting due to the blossoming cherries and bulbs. All the follies are highly decorated yet squarish, rough and angular – at odds with Richard's flowing Italianate style. Richard's decorative touch can be seen in the urns, the well and the classical touches such as the cherubs that stand among bluebells.

The large Portuguese Wall is the most elaborate garden folly. The Wall is about two metres high by ten metres long. A row of steps leads to a platform designed, it seems, simply to be walked up and over while meandering through the garden.

Basket designs appear often in Jim's mosaics. To many they are reminiscent of the traditional basket decorative motif on embroidery, frescos and wallpaper, but according to Jim they were supposed to be jewel boxes. The baskets sit beside motifs that include a broken "W", an ironic homage to the Westpac Bank logo. Richard has planted new azaleas in front of the Portuguese wall and ivy is becoming rampant. Although pretty, it may soon cover the facade. The large terracotta pots with embossed garlands which sit atop the Portuguese Wall are also Richard's additions, designed to give a more elegant feel to the scene.

Despite the difference in the brothers' decorative sense, there is an equilibrium and a balance in the garden. As Richard says, "Two minds are at work in this

garden". Jim and Richard Prentice have pursued their common dream of a spectacular and beautiful garden in a secret rainforest in the mountains. The "water feature" seems to symbolise their partnership. It has two ponds. The one on the left is decorated with Jim's mosaic work; a simple, more classic pair of cherubs sit on a shell above the pond on the right.

The Clover Gate leads us from the cottage to the house where the lunch table benches are on circular stone paving and two beautiful Burmese cats with eyes the yellow of mollis azaleas prowl beneath the four lawn mowers in the shed. The path passes an old water pump and there is a glimpse of a flute-playing cherub hiding in the fronds of a weeping silver birch. The horticultural achievements in this garden are paramount and indeed the spectacle in spring is extraordinary, made even more so by the permanent display of "Jim's Follies".

Cherub and horn...or Pan with his flute. The small statue set into the Portuguese Wall peeps out when the deciduous leaves have fallen.

The Moon Gate constructed by the Prentices from flat stones carted from Mt Tomah.

CASTLETHURSO

*If gentlemen still exist in Australia,
then they are probably
all to be found in Tasmania.*

Some gentlemen, like Captain John Gunn MBE, continue to live in manor estates or castles built by their ancestors. Captain Gunn's grandfather, F.J. Gunn, built the home Castlethurso in the 1880s at Low Head, a seaside town. According to Captain John Gunn, the family's *Norse ancestors were driven out of Thurso in the Scottish Highlands early last century and Castlethurso is named for the homeland. In Scandinavian mythology Thor was the God of thunder, Thurso is "God's river".*

This coast of Tasmania is heavily buffeted by westerly gales, known locally as the "roaring forties", that blow across the Pacific from South America. The salt-laden winds have a devastating effect on any garden, so protective hedges were devised. F.J. Gunn grew tall cypresses and clipped them into unusual leaning shapes, probably dictated largely by the prevailing winds as well as the height of ladders.

Captain John Gunn took up residence in the house in the 1970s and behind the shelter of these windbreaks has established a beautiful garden of flowering trees and shrubs with the additional help of a water supply from the town. Built as a retreat from a growing family and only lived in for many years as a holiday cottage, the house itself, true to tradition, takes the form of a castle. The topiary initials that grace the back wall are of F.J. Gunn's twin sons Andrew and Robert.

In this case the unusual hedges may appear to be eccentric follies but in truth are a practical defence against the elements and thus certainly no foolish invention.

Castles and Villages

*T*raditionally, European garden follies have always had a certain medieval, castellated quality. The numerous fake castles in the grounds of English landed gentry testify to the history of what has been called "Gothic Taste". The tradition continues in a modified and somewhat smaller form in Australian cottages where model villages replace castles. These are often nostalgic reminders of former countries and cultures.

At The Entrance, New South Wales, a large homage to this tradition sits on the front lawn, like a lost castle from a childhood fairytale. It is either a miniature medieval castle or, as the house is near the sea, perhaps a monster sand castle, or even a "fun palace" in the seaside amusement park tradition.

An austere brick house facade at The Entrance, New South Wales belies the regal dreams of the owner whose fantasy seaside castle has turrets, moat and drawbridge.

THE MODEL GARDEN

When nostalgia for the culture and memories of early life in a homeland far away becomes strong, many postwar immigrants display photographs of their country of birth, their town or city. Mr Jack Zuiderwyk went further. He built a complete Dutch village in his front garden to remind him of his birthplace.

Jack Zuiderwyk is now over 70. Born in The Hague, Holland, he left there in 1952 and brought his wife Tina and their four children to Australia. After almost 20 years working as a painter, Jack Zuiderwyk retired and it was then that the longing to see his native country took hold. It seemed an impossibly forlorn hope that he would ever see the familiar streets and buildings of Holland again.

With time on his hands and a remarkable ability, Mr Zuiderwyk set about compensating for his nostalgia by creating a complete Dutch village square in his garden. Houses were made one by one, commencing with a windmill. Village streets soon appeared around the central pump where miniature people gathered daily to draw water. Each individual was dressed in nineteenth-century costumes similar to those worn in Holland until early this century.

My Dutch village has turned heads for 14 years. People ask me why but I don't know why I made it.

The most important thing is patience. Everything is handmade, handmade cement bricks and timber. I've never had any vandals or thieves because people like my village.

Structures in the village include two windmills, a church and a clock tower, horse-drawn carts and a miniature fishing pond. The central town hall is copied from the real one in Gouda, the town famous for its cheese. For inspiration Jack used his large personal

Jack Zuiderwyk with the last remaining windmill from his Dutch village at Corrimal, New South Wales. The windmill has turned, and so have heads, for 14 years.

A group of authentic village houses with figures dressed by Tina Zuiderwyk.

collection of photographs, magazines and postcards. His wife Tina made the costumes, largely from memory and a thorough knowledge of Dutch history.

Each morning of his retirement, at 8 a.m. Jack Zuiderwyk would enter the workshop under his house and remain there steadily until 4 p.m., making building after building, figure after figure. Everything sat outside – rain, hail or shine – but conservation was not a problem to Jack. If anything became a little shabby he simply replaced it; it would have been too hard to take them in and put them out each day.

I've never had to worry about things getting dirty. I just left everything out all the time and then every year I paint everything up. Some figures were six to eight years old. I found my village was the best reminder of Holland. Also, when I made my village, then I didn't have to cut the grass again.

In time newspapers and television stations came to hear of the miraculous appearance of a miniature Holland in the suburb of Woonona. At least four news reports were made. After one such report which explained that due to financial constraints Jack and Tina would never be able to fulfil their nostalgia for their home country, the Dutch Airline KLM gave the couple free return tickets to Holland – achieving much publicity not only for KLM but also for Mr and Mrs Zuiderwyk's garden.

Today the Zuiderwyk's village is represented by a single windmill which still turns happily in the wind. The remaining structures and people have been stored pending installation of the village square in the Dutch Village for the Aged, planned for the district. One windmill turns alone as a testament to the complete village which once stood there. Although Mr Zuiderwyk's sight is now somewhat impaired, he greets visitors interested in his garden with warmth and pleasure, showing them the various videos he has of the garden in its former glory.

CANBERRA'S VILLAGE GREEN

Making things in miniature is often thought of as a trivial hobby, closely connected to childish pursuits, like keeping dolls' houses complete with all miniature domestic equipment – yet it has fascinated many for centuries.

The theme of nostalgia for the home country or for the grandeur of places visited is occasionally expressed in miniature in unusual gardens throughout Australia.

Australia is home to several historic model villages giving views of life in other parts of the world. Depending on their size and scale, some are opened to visitors. One such development is Cockington Green in Canberra, which began as a domestic garden conceived and designed by Doug Sarah and members of his family. Named after the small village of Cockington in Devon, the concept took shape after visiting a similar model village during a trip to England in 1972. Most of the buildings are small-scale replicas made from photographs. Thousands of miniature people, animals and birds are placed in the gardens that surround the "village", each grouping depicting daily life earlier

this century. The buildings include the village inn (a replica of one in Cheshire), five buildings in the village of Cockington, the village green complete with a cricket match, an oast house, thatched cottage and village church.

Most of the buildings are constructed of cement sheeting, fibreglass and steel. Despite their appearance very little timber has been used because of its slow disintegration when exposed to the elements. Resin and ceramics as well as thousands of small bricks have also been used.

This garden is far from minimal maintenance; it requires continual tending. It can never become too established as the shrubs all grow too large to suit their location and have to be removed so that up to 20 per cent of the plants in the garden are replaced each year. Lawn maintenance is also a continuous preoccupation as the owners try to simulate the ideal rolling green lawns of English countryside.

The Sarah family has opened the garden to the public and take pride in the appreciation of their creation. Maintaining these artworks can be costly, so entrance fees are put to good use.

Among the green lawns of Canberra, the Lilliputian recreation of the English village of Cockington is complete with miniature plantings. Like Gulliver, visitors must step carefully near the village people.

Cactus Gardens

The otherworldly trifid shapes of many cacti make them logical choices for gardeners who want to create an unusual display. Cacti shapes alone make them worth the effort of gardening and when they bring forth spectacular blooms, they are often the talk of the neighbourhood.

Some gardeners set out a tall array along the boundary of the front garden. Like spiky palings they seem to protect those inside and to deter invaders. An odd planting custom is still common in country areas where a tall tubular cactus is planted within a circular object. Favourites are disused car tyres, farm machinery or even old cement mixers. The association of the plants with arid environments suggests their partnership with barren corners of the garden and many are placed in pebble gardens or set among stones, driftwood and other dry objects.

Hollywood's Wild West movies took hold of popular imagination for many decades in Australia. Garden decoration grew around centrepieces of prickly pear. Like branches of ovoid green dinner plates, they spread across the Australian environment in pest proportions until brought under biological control. Some are still grown for their fruit.

The cactus garden as a genre probably had its heyday in the 1950s and 1960s. However a few remnant rambling examples remain in which bizarre and spectacular plant varieties complement a myriad of other eclectic forms of garden decoration.

Joseph Lowry's spectacular cactus garden ruins at Port Wakefield, west of Adelaide.

CROWN OF THORNS

One large cactus garden outside Adelaide has been known to several generations.

Standing beside the main western highway, its tall spiky cacti beckon like a lost city of sentinels among which flashes of statuary peek at fast passing cars.

Driving west from Adelaide, a four-lane highway heads past car sales yards, piles of old tyres and truck and car graveyards. The road is noisy and oppressive and an array of roadside eating joints beckon including some like McDonalds and Hungry Jacks which would be at home in the American southwest – in keeping with the original home of many of the cacti.

Beyond the industrial area the road passes through small market garden holdings, olive groves and fruit trees. The road is clogged with heavy transport vehicles and holiday caravans. After about an hour it levels out and a wide flat plain (that feels somewhat like the Nullarbor) heads west to the distant horizon. The roadside is occasionally decorated by dead animals – rabbits,

Joseph Lowry's religious zeal ensured his garden had a brooding atmosphere like the cactus version of Gethsemane. The painted finishes on the classical statuary below are by Mr Schoff, the caretaker.

birds, reptiles and sometimes a dingo.

The small towns along the way consist of a single store selling petrol, a church, small-scale sheep farms, abandoned old stone houses and barns. Once in a while the front yard of a house is ornamented with a cactus plant, a Mexican figure or a white cement bird, a hint that more exciting things are in store. Then the vision emerges. An apparition perhaps. A low stone wall extends for a hundred metres backed by a spectacular fence of red hot pokers which leads to an entrance gate guarded by two giant brightly-painted cement lions. These seem to lie like temple watchdogs before the shrine within. And then the centrepiece appears – the giant decapitated head of Jesus, 50 times larger than human scale, surrounded by

The altar fireplace, gateway to another realm.

Prehistoric painted tree forms, light fittings and cacti suggest the torment and mental unrest of a wildly expressionist, reclusive garden artist.

numerous cacti. In older photographs of this garden, an immense sculpture of Flora (the Roman goddess of flowers) stood guard nearby in an abundant array of cacti, statuary and garden ornaments.

The elaborate 13-acre garden was made in the 1940s and 1950s by Joseph Reginald Lowry, a devout man who collected unusual examples of cacti from all over the world. Although somewhat reclusive, hiding whenever visitors called, he attended the small church in the nearby town of Windsor all his life.

It can take half an hour to walk through the stone-lined circular paths and avenues throughout the property. Rounding each corner is a different vignette: a Japanese lantern near a cypress tree, Mexican figures – some freshly painted, others peeling and decaying – cement pillars, giant figures and urns. One display has a collection of turkey platters and other remnants of past feasts.

The current caretaker is Karl Schoff, Joseph Lowry having long since departed the garden. Mr Schoff has an uphill battle maintaining the acreage, restoring the gardens and repainting figurines that are peeling or broken as the garden is almost impossible to secure due to its visibility and long frontage on the highway. Over the years of neglect since Mr Lowry's departure, many porcelain urns, jugs and plates dating back to earlier this century which were collected and put in place by Mr Lowry have been broken or damaged so that only a rough visual approximation of the original garden remains.

Rounding each bend in the phallic forest a new garden appears. A sunken cactus garden in the centre is surrounded by taller protective bushes followed by a shrine-like presentation complete with painted driftwood, inlaid crockery and large urns. Italianate compositions of young girls in drapes are Mr Schoff's favourites. Whether out of a sense of propriety and modesty or out of concern for the effect of cactus prickles on naked flesh, Mr Schoff has coated the bodies of the classical figurines with blue paint to simulate clothing – sometimes to odd effect, like a cold Venus in a wet suit. The faces have been left white like their marble antecedents and some of the female figures are permitted bare arms. Until recently a beautiful young female figure holding a bunch of grapes welcomed visitors to the pond. She was painted blue suggesting a dress but in her original state she was less modest. Her charms attracted kidnappers and she has since left the garden where she had lived for over 10 years.

Another classical maiden playing her lyre welcomes visitors. Her hair is black, so she is definitely of Mediterranean origin, however the paintwork suggests she too might be wearing a wetsuit and diver's boots, and carrying a towel.

This garden has a truly fantastic array of cacti imported by Mr Lowry. The South Australian Cactus Society visits regularly and takes samples and cuttings to propagate elsewhere.

There is no formality in design, the entire arrangement being much like a jumbled domestic array, each little scene having its own personal raison d'être, the significance of which is now lost. On large gnarled pieces of painted tree roots and driftwood, figures sit, stand, rest or peep out of the crevices and hollows.

Light fittings, disused kitchen equipment and other discarded objects are also used in the decoration of this bizarre garden.

It is clear that Joseph Lowry's

thoughts were often on the Almighty and his handmade inscription on a cement plaque is well preserved, serving as a fitting epitaph.

The kiss of the sun for pardon
The song of the birds for mirth
You are nearer God's heart in the garden
Than anywhere else on earth.

Mr Schoff's garden restoration suggests this could be Venus in her wetsuit with bath towel and lyre, stepping gingerly among the prickles.

WHEN SINGING OUR
PRAISES OF
PROGRESS IN YEARS
TRY AND REMEMBER
THE OLD PIONEERS

THE KISS OF THE SUN FOR P
THE SONG OF THE BIRDS FOR
YOU ARE NEARER GOD'S HEART IN
THAN ANYWHERE ELSE ON E

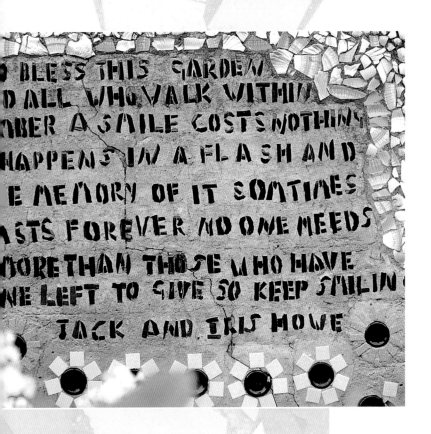

O BLESS THIS GARDEN
D ALL WHO WALK WITHIN
BER A SMILE COSTS NOTHING
HAPPENS IN A FLASH AND
E MEMORY OF IT SOMTIMES
STS FOREVER NO ONE NEEDS
MORE THAN THOSE WHO HAVE
NE LEFT TO GIVE SO KEEP SMILIN
TACK AND IRIS HOWE

A Word or Two from the Maker

Mottos to live by,
homilies to hold dear
and words of wisdom for
the weary, all set in cement
to contemplate in the
garden.

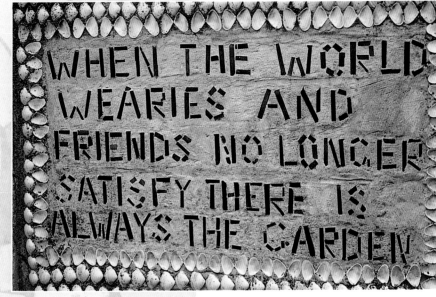

WHEN THE WORLD
WEARIES AND
FRIENDS NO LONGER
SATISFY THERE IS
ALWAYS THE GARDEN

Classics

*T*he first sign that the Gods of Ancient Rome and Greece still rule the lives of mere mortals can be the appearance of artichoke-like fruit or pine cones on top of fence pillars and balustrades, or an array of Doric, Ionic or Corinthian columns along a fence or house facade. Like the gnomes, pixies and Disney characters that people many gardens, their celestial equivalents – cherubs and seraphs, nymphs and Arcadian gods – are strategically placed in numerous others.

It is common to guard the entrance in some way. Lions predominate. Fierce and majestic, they give a regal air to the abode, as do equal favourites, eagles. Australiana parodies of these are occasionally seen using kangaroos or even galahs.

Venus descends outback where spinach is the food of love.

HOME OF THE GODS

Opposite his workshop in northern Adelaide, Ferdie Zaltron's home is surrounded by a brightly-painted blue and red wall surmounted by huge white classical figures.

A semi-naked Goddess of Love, probably Aphrodite, seems to wantonly beckon, elbows raised, hands behind her head, but her guards are not as approachable. Their ancient Greek and Roman progenitors are unknown but the heritage is obvious in the emperor's stance and the musculature of athletes and warriors. Flora, the Goddess of Flowers who once ornamented victors at the Roman Games with a garland, now greets visitors to the Zaltron property in the same way.

In many houses classical sculptures lend a European or Italianate aura, perhaps reminding their owners of former homes, or the grander villas in their childhood towns or villages. To others they simply denote an increase in status, even the presence of taste, showing that classicism is for the upwardly mobile. The gardens of Italy and Europe are all homes to figures of the Olympian gods, so why not those of mere mortals? Every garden supply shop offers well-known examples: the peeing cherub fountain, the diaphanously semi-robed young damsel holding a basket of fruit or a dish of flowers on her head, or Venus.

Many simply love these modern copies of their classical ancestors for their physique, facial beauty and romantic posture and feel they lend a touch of high culture to the most prosaic of gardens. Modern mass-produced classical garden statuary is designed for domestic gardens. The figures are seldom exact copies of the ancient originals but have been modified and prettied up, sometimes with a touch of romanticism. In Ancient Rome, drapery and mantles were often used to give the figure breadth and power. In modern equivalents this has been reduced to a vestige of its former self as coquettish female figures hold flimsy small coverings – or let them slip. The originals were once highly painted, chiefly red and gold and although some modern gardeners paint their figures, most of today's classic figure fanciers prefer to leave them white, simulating the marble originals.

The very rich import these solid Italian originals, while others buy copies from manufacturers such as Ferdie Zaltron.

The gods of Olympia aloft along Ferdie Zaltron's front wall. Aphrodite, Zeus and their companions seem to beckon mere mortals inside.

FADING PHOENICIA

The house and garden of Matthew Cordina recall the famous Hotel Phoenicia in the centre of Valetta, Malta.

Matthew Cordina's "Hotel Phoenicia" was home to many Maltese seamen who came to Port Kembla.

The gateway of the Flagstaff Road home is guarded by two cement lions seated near urns, suggesting a Mediterranean decorative sense – but most significantly on either side are two crests: one of the Maltese Cross and the other of a Knight. Together they flag the presence of a Maltese villa on the edge of Port Kembla, the steel lungs of Australia.

Within the walled front courtyard one steps immediately on to a crazy mosaic patio of cut tiles in pink and blue pastels. Another world unfolds. This beautiful garden villa, now sadly past its zenith, has fallen into disrepair yet still entrances. Matthew Cordina whispers "Romeo and Juliet" to visitors who gaze enthralled at his mosaic castle of turrets, stairs and interior courtyard balconies.

In the forecourt, a terraced garden area surrounds a well and fish ponds. All are paved with handmade mosaic work made 14 years ago by Matthew Cordina and his brother-in-law, Tony Azzopardi. The house of cement blocks descends the hillside so that the rear section is several stories high. This is topped with a tower and a turreted roof area, also decorated with cut tile mosaic surfaces. An internal walled courtyard is surrounded by balconies and steps decorated in what Mr Cordina calls the Phoenician style.

We are Phoenicians and that's why we make this house and this garden. All the houses were built like this there – villas. They have big garden and ground. At the bottom there was another one there, it was beautiful. It was all full of ferns and everything, orchids.

Maltese gardens don't have cracked tiles like mine, but they have rocks. Not good soil like here – all like dust. But they make it grow, begonias, dahlias, poppies, beautiful poppies – red, pink, white. In Malta there are poppies all over the place and geraniums, beautiful geraniums. They have them on the walls, everywhere. When I came here, I was dying for a garden. I love gardens.

I start the garden myself, the way I wanted it. It was beautiful. The pool was full of big fish, like trout. Beautiful fish, they were everywhere. And there was a bird cage full of birds. Beautiful birds.

Matthew Cordina, who made the garden and its decorations, was born in

Malta and brought up during wartime in a very poor family of 11 children. When he was only 14 he joined the navy and suffered one of many traumas he endured throughout his life when the ship was blown up. When he returned to Malta he found his father had already died, so he was taken in to live with his sister and then travelled on to London.

From London he heard from his sister, Nina Azzopardi, who was then living with her husband Tony in Port Kembla. So he joined his sister and her new family to "help her to make a home and family in the proper way". The Azzopardi–Cordina families all worked as labourers in the coal and steel industries of Wollongong and Port Kembla. For a period the Azzopardis boarded itinerant seamen and the house was extended to offer single rooms for the men calling at Port Kembla on short or long stays.

The design of the house and garden is unique. Its embellishments include the cement well in the forecourt and many large urns covered with stucco cement flowers, all of which were handmade and painted by the two men. Classical figures are strategically placed around the garden. A girl with a water pitcher kneels beside the now abandoned fish pond and a young boy offers a platter of fruit in another corner of the garden. Guarding every gateway are various figures including the Virgin Mary, Patroness of Sailors.

The Azzopardis clearly built this house on the Lake Heights hill in the style of the forts and castles of the Knights of St John in Valletta, the capital of Malta. Mount Sciberras, on

The entrance to Phoenicia has various gateway guardians including two Maltese crests, symbolising the Knights of Malta.

The Romeo and Juliet mosaic stairways lead to both dungeons and high turreted balconies of Phoenicia.

"The Grand Masters". This dwelling had majestic gates, and tiers and battlements which have been imitated in the Azzopardi home. Another building in Valletta evoked by the Azzopardi–Cordina home now houses government departments. This Middle Eastern style structure is built around courtyards containing fountains and is edged with an open colonnade. It is a multi-storey building and one courtyard contains a statue of King Neptune. Around Neptune are palm trees, hibiscus, fern and a jacaranda tree – plantings repeated in the Azzopardi–Cordina garden.

The front garden of the house is edged with palm trees as is Valetta's Hotel Phoenicia. The main bar has replicas of suits of armour used during the Great Siege – the Azzopardi family room has a bar and freestanding suit of armour. Tapestries cover the walls of the Hotel Phoenicia's main restaurant, as they do in the dining room of the Azzopardi house.

The interior of the Azzopardi–Cordina house is a remarkably preserved ornate display of marble and gilded objects, furniture and decorative features. The house is a historic example of transportation of the decorative culture and social elements of Maltese life to another part of the world. All furniture and objects have been shipped to Australia bit by bit, including the stuffed peacock which emulates a phoenix in the family room, as the Azzopardis began to make their fortune through their own sweat and labour in the postwar immigrant exodus to Australia. "Phoenicia" may be fading but it is still phantastic.

top of which Valletta is built, has many lateral streets which slope down precipitously to the water, just like the rear of the Azzopardi house. The Valletta houses are stepped with overhanging balconies. The Knights of St John found fertile soil on Malta which produced vegetables and fruits, orchards with figs, pomegranates and orange trees. The most imposing residence was that of

CELESTIAL ORCHESTRA

Squeezed between the compacted small houses of inner Sydney, up an alley only one person's width, is the home of artist David Humphries.

In his tiny interior courtyard, Humphries has created a secret haven.

A high brick wall creates privacy for the water garden within. On top of the wall, a group of Bernini cherubs have descended to play their lyre, violin, trumpet, cello and cymbals for the mortals below in this secret abode. David had the brightly-painted cherubs made from old moulds.

The entire floor of the courtyard is a pond for golden koi, miniature turtles, exotic flowering ginger, black bamboo and water lilies. The appearance of the angels along the skyline of rooftops, television aerials and inner city high rise flats is Humphries' creative gift – more often seen in the public art works (mainly terrazzo floors and murals) he makes for high-profile buildings.

Unlike other quirky gardeners who decorate front gardens for all to see, David Humphries ensures that while his mainstream art works are all in the public eye, his garden remains an "angelic" place of privacy.

Perched among rooftops and television aerials, a group of cherubs alights to play for mortals and the golden koi below.

Gnome Man's Land

To some international visitors, the ubiquitous Australian garden gnome glimpsed from a passing tourist bus is a mysterious object. Placed strategically in many gardens, they seem prevalent enough to suggest a religious significance, or at least an ancient Australian cultural tradition, much like the small stone lanterns found near water in neatly organised traditional Japanese gardens. In Australia, they are clearly connected to the medieval European belief in fairies, goblins, pixies and elves.

"Little people" inhabit numerous Australian domestic gardens. Most are commonly called gnomes and are bought from garden retailers. Some are handmade, and these are probably the most interesting examples of gnome garden folk art. In the more elaborately developed personal spaces where they dwell, the gardener usually constructs themes and groupings, and occasionally a complete environment for these small denizens of the garden. Common surroundings thought to suit gnomes include cacti, pebbled areas, painted rock borders and enclosures of some kind from which they peep – like a garden zoo. In more verdant tropical areas the pond or water garden is where lady frogs in swimsuits imitate "Miss Froggy went a courting".

A common though unlikely scene in many of these Australian spaces is the Mexican peasant: driving his donkey, pulling his cart or dozing under his sombrero. He usually appears in an austere environment, often associated with cactus – in a simulation of the desert from which he is thought to have come. Gnomes can also pop up in surprisingly tasteful locations, adding a touch of whimsy to an otherwise conventional garden.

A rash of garden gnomes followed the release of Walt Disney movies, particularly *Bambi*, and *Snow White and the Seven Dwarfs*. Bambi deer can still be bought in garden supply shops.

But gnomes inhabited Australian gardens long before Walt Disney produced his movies and the earlier examples in good order are now prized possessions of a select club of gnome fanciers. They augment their collections by kidnapping the little people from the gardens of those they feel don't appreciate them, sometimes leaving messages behind in their place.

Gnome Woodstock. The little people en masse, perhaps assembling before the invasion.

BOSS AND THE LITTLE PEOPLE

Allan Hewitt's gnome garden is famous in Goulburn, New South Wales. It once won second prize in the Lilac Time garden competition, although its best feature was not lilac, but "little people" who had been busy usurping plants.

Allan Hewitt's front garden corral – designed more to curb the denizens' tendency to roam than to prevent theft.

No doubt the judges were somewhat bemused by this garden's entry, but thought that its unique qualities might attract visitors to the town. Allan Hewitt and his mother Elsie, who "looks after the inside", are delighted with the interest shown on garden open days.

Almost every archetypal cement figure is present in the groupings Allan has arranged within zoo-like enclosures. A few years ago, most of the characters were out the front but the gnome kleptomaniacs struck and now only those that can be cemented in remain there, the others having retreated to safer ground.

A lot more now are out the back. It pays you to cement them in. What's left at the front now is cemented down so they'd be flat out getting them.

Under the formal archway entrance to the house, the steps and foreground

All have to be painted each year as do the colourful stone borders around the garden.

As well as organising the garden vignettes and seeing to the arrangements of cement figures, Allan also grows roses and flowering shrubs which give his environment a cottage garden feel. From the street the colour and life within evoke childhood stories. The onlooker can be sure that a kindly person who enjoys fantasy lives in this house. In the middle of the lawn, like the ringmaster strategically positioned beneath a weeping rose, one gnome stands firmly, his feet planted apart with an air of authority. He is labelled the "boss". Allan Hewitt is confident that when his attention is elsewhere his "boss" will take over and maintain order among the garden citizens.

The garden has occupied most of Allan's working life. Although he has worked at part-time jobs from time to time, the garden has been his passion.

I didn't work very much in my life, just odd jobs. I'm 64 years old now and about 30 years or so ago, I thought "oh well, I can't get the work so I'll start the garden". Some of the jobs I've had have been moving second-hand furniture, working in the market garden, or collecting eggs from chooks and so on. I love doing the garden, I could spend all night out there, getting an idea of what to do next. It keeps me busy every day, getting the weeds out, taking the leaves from the pebbles and cutting the lawn which I trim right around with the grass shears.

The miniature environments Allan has created within his enclosures are

have been carpeted with imitation lawn so that the area can be swept clean to show off the figurines at their best. A formal reception committee, standing to attention, is assembled on the steps. Each character appears to represent one of the main "gnome grouping" constituents: Bambi is there on behalf of Disneyland, a lost goddess represents Olympia, a lion for the gate guardians, and Australian selections – the kangaroo and an Aboriginal figure.

At the front door, a reception committee repesents all the garden ornament constituents.

reminiscent of nineteenth-century museum displays of flora and fauna. The characters move through the jungle or undergrowth, peer from bushes and stand protected behind their enclosures, unable to escape.

When I made the fenced off area, I just took it in to my head putting things here and there then my mother said it looked good, and I thought "Yes, that looks great". The white pebbles came from Goulburn nursery. I've certainly spent a lot of money but I've got something to show anyway.

The cement figures were collected on many interstate visits, driving long distances to see relatives. Favourite sources were a shop with gnomes in Birchip, Victoria and an aunt in Queensland who found the donkeys with their carts.

For the Hewitts, hanging the washing

Under his standard rose in the centre of the yard, "boss" gnome keeps everyone in order.

is difficult as, sheltering beneath the Hills Hoist, two large white swan planters have been befriended by two sleepy Mexicans and a yellow duck. Behind them, stretching around the fence perimeter, are neatly arranged gardens of rocks and shrubs. The white brick edging encloses a wishing well near which the two donkeys who appear to have strayed from their Mexican masters are now befriended by older indigenous inhabitants of the landscape. Under the bushes opposite, majestic white lions rest beside "puppy dogs", frogs and "pussy cats".

CUDDLY GNOMES OF CUNDLETOWN

Beside the main road in Cundletown, on the north coast of New South Wales, Eileen O'Brien has created a haven for many small friends – gnomes, white ladies, frogs, cement animals and one plastic lobster.

A great many gnomes have moved into the mushroom homes provided by Eileen O'Brien throughout her garden.

The garden display in the front garden is dominated by a tall white female figure posed amidst a group of brightly painted characters standing sociably near their bright red mushroom home.

I have a few white ladies. One is Venus de Milo, you know, the goddess of love. She's next to the archway. The other one is just a Chinese Lady. Years and years ago, my daughter-in-law and I were at the nursery and there were three broken ones lying there. I asked the lady what she was going to do with them, so she sold them to me for $15. I brought them home, had a hole drilled down through them for a support rod, then we painted them. They've been there every since, about 12 years.

Just as fairies are thought to live beneath mushrooms, and the appearance of a ring of toadstools after rain has signalled to many children the presence of fairies in their garden, it seems that gnomes prefer giant red mushrooms – especially in Mrs O'Brien's garden.

The mushrooms, well, I've got various mushrooms. I bought a lot of them – little ones, and of course I have a mushroom house for the gnomes. The

in Mrs O'Brien's garden have different personalities. Now widowed, she finds comfort in her small companions' friendship and enjoys the great deal of interest from passing motorists, who often stop to take photographs and admire the array in the garden.

Well, being on the main road, I do have people stop and look and neighbours have said to me, "are you selling your house?" and I say "no", "oh well, somebody must be taking photos". I often had that happen. There was one car that took my fence down, only a portion of it, but I ended up getting enough money from it to put a brick and lattice fence up in front which really makes it, because now I can plant right along the back of the fence and let them grow up. I don't think he was busy looking at the gnomes – because it was about 1 o'clock in the morning.

On one side of the garden Eileen and Max created a water scene, complete with "beavers", gnomes and an array of unconnected ornaments. In the foreground is a gnome dressed in football clothes but his presence in a

mushroom house is near the Chinese Lady. I did that at ceramics. A lady has classes in Taree and her husband makes the moulds. The clay is white looking stuff and then we rub it back and then work on it with special little knives and things. We paint them and they are fired, and then we glaze them, and they're fired again, and then they're finished. I mentioned to my husband Max that I'd like some big mushrooms

out the back and when I came home from work a few days later, he had mushrooms made out of fibreglass with cement stalks – I suppose one would be two feet high, you know, a round sort of old-fashioned washer dish on top, and another was like a stool, but it's a mushroom.

All the characters

"Miss Froggy goes a courting."

"They've got their eyes shut because they've been standing there that long guarding their house and they've got sleepy."

photograph of the garden surprised Mrs O'Brien.

I've never noticed him. They don't always stay in the same place, year in and year out, you know. At different times I fix the garden up and then I change one from the front and put it at the back. I've more or less got a changing garden. He's just come from somewhere. There are times I think of a gnome and I think "Now where's he gone, has somebody taken him, or what happened to him?" Then I find that I've put him somewhere. At 70 years old I suppose the memory does go a bit, and I think, "How did he get there?"

But then there are other people like me who really love gnomes, they really think that gnomes move. They do, yes! Some of them have a little dell down the back yard, covered with trees and the gnomes are all in this area, and they really believe that after dark, when everything settles down, the gnomes go places, and are back by morning. I don't know myself about that, but I look for a certain gnome, you know, that I haven't seen for a long time and I can't find him.

Eileen was born just across the street from where she now lives in Cundletown. Her parent's small house is still there.

I think it would be a heritage home now. It's plank. As a little child my parents shifted to Sydney and I lived in Surry Hills for about ten years, then they shifted to Mascot, but after that we came back here to live with my grandfather straight opposite where I live now. Then my Dad bought the block of land where I live and built the house that I live in. I suppose it

would be about 48 years old.

Eileen married and moved to Taree where she brought up two of her three children alone, earning her living as cook first in a private hospital and then in the Taree Prime Hospital. She and her second husband, Max, moved to the present house 14 years ago.

Max was very artistic and he started off tiling pots each side of the archway one wet day. We got some terracotta pots and we cut tiles and we used to go to the beach and gather shells and we glued them all on. And then we started making stepping stones, fixing up the house and the pond.

Eileen loves gnomes and prefers them to the more expensive equivalents chosen by some of her relatives.

My brother, yes, he likes things like garden ornaments, but he went in for big expensive things that cost hundreds of dollars. My niece goes in for the big Venus de Milo and one of the other goddesses, you know, with the cape draped around her and that, but I've never been into that sort of thing. Everything's on the cheap because you know, I bought and paid for the house I've lived in, furnished it as it is which is quite beautiful inside. They're wealthy people and I'm not.

But it's not only just that, I love them. It's just my love for gnomes. I'd like to have a little garden just specially for gnomes. I can see it in my brain but I can't describe it. I can look at a gnome and I don't want to buy it, and I can look at another gnome and I have to take it home. I've got one little gnome – he's pushing a wheelbarrow. That's an ideal thing to set in a garden, you know,

In Eileen's water scene, the lobster lives in the water; the little people have the choice of Japanese lantern or shoe shelters as they leave their mushroom homes.

ready to work. I don't know, I can't explain it. It's just that I've always liked them. They're sweet, they are beautiful, lovable.

Many of Eileen's garden characters have been presents from loved ones. Max bought her the giant kangaroo that sits beside the porch he built with its handtiled decoration. Max and her son also contributed many of the mushrooms and some of the smaller characters as well.

Her grandson has also been involved in the development of the garden and all the family admire her efforts.

My grandson, he came up, he was about 15 at the time, and we cleaned the garden all up, we made it beautiful – it was a credit to us, and when he finished along the Taree side fence, I was inside getting an icy cold drink, and when I came out Gary said "those rabbits that you had sitting on the path, Nan, see where I've put them?" "Oh, that's lovely Gaz, that's just what I was thinking of doing." And exactly where he put them, that's what I was going to do. He put them over under some trees.

You see, when everything is out in flower and you have a bare patch, you automatically think, now I'll shift that bloke from up the back and put him there, and put this here. I've got frogs, I love frogs, so I might think, yes, the frogs will go there, and then you fill the bare patch up with them.

Eileen sometimes mentions the passing of the years and gives the impression that it is the older gnomes she likes most. Two very old cracked and peeling gnomes have been mended.

They're so old that you'd normally put them in the garbage, but I can't bring myself to – it's just that I've had them a long time and they've been a lot of places in the garden.

The old gnomes are like garden guardians to Eileen O'Brien. Two in particular evoke Walt Disney characters, either Sleepy or Dopey. They stand beside their mushroom home holding daisies, eyes closed, sound asleep. Eileen will soon have additional help guarding the house. In addition to two gnome brothers at either end of the front porch, she plans to erect white Egyptian heads on top of the gate posts.

Spot the Dog

*Making memorials to
the family dog or cat –
a pet foible of many
eccentric gardeners.*

Guardians of the Garden Outback

*I*n the 1950s a popular cement figurine was an Aboriginal man complete with spear and boomerang. Some even carried a lizard for lunch. Hundreds of gardens throughout Australia announced their unique heritage with an outback guardian, suitably attired and ready to defend the domestic territory with spear and shield. They were all stereotypical figures, in keeping with other such iconic images in these gardens: the Mexican peasant in his sombrero, Snow White and the Dwarfs, giant kangaroos, emus and pelicans were equal favourites.

Aboriginal figures were invariably placed in environments that suited their owners' concept of the bush, desert or jungle as the case might be. Freshly painted figurines would appear either as mysterious inhabitants of dells in the bottom of the garden (like fairies) or stand proudly against the corrugated iron fence in an arid dune-like landscape symbolic of the outback. They were Australia's version of "Black Sambo" and pointed uncomfortably to the naive assumptions of many of their owners that they were proudly displaying their Australianness by having their own "pet" blackfellow in the garden.

Scratch a quirky garden these days, or rather part the leaves, and one still finds black-skinned denizens guarding remote corners. They are often much-loved members of the family, albeit silent and concrete. These native inhabitants are respectful towards their owners, do not answer back, demand land rights or claim discrimination. Their owners, unchallenged, often feel proud of the patriotic Australian attitude they are displaying.

For as long as these "native" figures have existed, most Aborigines have regarded them with loathing, seeing them as dangerous and derogatory stereotypes which promulgate an old Australian racist concept. Today, however, in the wake of significant political gains there is a more relaxed attitude among some, even an appropriation of the parody itself.

In Bairnsdale, Victoria, an Aboriginal-owned business repairs the broken cement figures of the original indigenous Australian "little people". The Aboriginal presence in a suburban street in another country town in western New South Wales is flagged by these old Australian icons, now reunited with their own people, in the front yard of the local Aboriginal co-op.

Archetypal garden guardians in their "natural" settings: corrugated iron and tree stumps for noble warriors, desert cacti and pebbles for Mexican peasants.

NURIOOTPA NOMADS

Beside the main tourist drive from Adelaide to the Barossa Valley sits the house of Mr Florenz Nuske, its entrance marked by an immense wine bottle, a souvenir from one of the floats in the Barossa Valley Wine Festival.

The fantastic world of Florenz Nuske.

Mr Nuske, a descendent of early Prussian emigrants to the Barossa Valley, is now a well-known plumber in the district of Nuriootpa, a famous wine-growing area. Mr Nuske likes to keep anything old. His treasures stay in the shed for a while until he finds a place for them among the other garden inhabitants – numerous cement objects, animals and sculptures.

In the centre of the garden is an elaborate water construction. A huge

Aboriginal figure stands beside it, poised ready to spear a fish – or he could be contemplating the giant crocodile that waits on the rocks near the pond. Water-loving birds and animals are arranged around the scene and Mr Nuske's plumbing skills have resurrected an old water pump from which water flows once its handle is cranked.

It's a water scene, everything that goes with water. Birds, crocodiles, old pelicans. The large Aboriginal man came from New South Wales. He is supposed to be an Islander. He was made by a nursery supplier and I bought it from a shop for about $200. The other scene, that's the Aboriginal collection. Some of the little ones have got stolen and I haven't been able to replace them. But that's supposed to depict an early Aboriginal settlement.

Beside the water scene, a group of Aboriginal figures is posed before a humpy. The arrangement used to have a fire that glowed whenever Mr Nuske turned it on, like the nativity scenes that grace lawns in other areas at Christmas. The environment is thoroughly peopled – an inhabitant peeps from every branch and every crevice of tree stumps. Various gnomes assemble in tree hollows. For security reasons Mr Nuske has embedded many in a concrete base or wired them to the ground.

You put them there and they steal them so you've got to cement them down. They even break them off. The big mushrooms have been broken but they can't take them because they've got a steel rod in them half way down. I used to have cactus all along the front but they would just get a knife as they

*went along and snap them off so I gave
that away.*

Mr Nuske has been collecting all the
garden paraphernalia for 20 years,
travelling around Australia racing go-
carts. Whenever he saw something
unusual he'd pick it up. Carrying the go-
cart in the trailer, he had plenty of room
to cart it back to the Barossa Valley.
Now Mr Nuske and his wife travel
widely on the ballroom dance circuit so
are able to add to their collection of
cement figurines along the way.

*We do a lot of dancing – old vogue,
new vogue. Once a week at least,
sometimes twice a week. We go away
every weekend, we're never home so I
haven't had time to do much in the
garden. Soon I'll settle down and do a
bit more. Dig up some more garden, put
beds there and ornaments around them.
I made the garden mainly because I
went travelling and you'd see something
and pick it up and it just grew from
there. I've got old butter churns, old
cots, things you can't get any more, like
the old pump. They used to be
household pumps years ago, you can't
buy them. Some figures came from as
far away as Geelong, others from the
coal fields at Leigh Creek, others from
New South Wales, from West Wyalong,
and many others from places closer to
Nuriootpa. A few I got from the Italian
on the Anzac Highway, 30 years ago or
more and another I won in a raffle, that
one over there, the dog. The giraffe
came from Kapunda. There's a chap
there who used to make them but they
are out of business now and not made
any more.*

I made a garden like this just because

The front yard has a working pump where every water-loving bird and animal comes to drink.

I thought I'd like something like that. I was interested in bits and pieces. Something unusual. Yes, it just grew. I can't tell you how it began. First I got an old log and some dwarfs and put them around. It's just a hobby I picked up and I've been doing it here for about 40 years I suppose. Before that I lived up the river, 30 miles away, so I haven't come very far. I try to keep everything together if I can, things that go together.

There are things here that would be anything in excess of a hundred years old. Three generations ago, concrete and metal. I've wired them together now so they are too heavy to take away. But the mushroom I made myself with cast wire and cement.

His garden is not finished yet; the shed is full of objects waiting to be put on display when the dancing circuit permits.

Nuriootpa nativity scene, erected by Florenz Nuske as a reminder of the district's Aboriginal heritage.

Fences, Defences and Wonderful Walls

People mark their boundaries in many ways. Dogs, of course, use trees to stake out their territory, whereas humans, in general, tend to build structures, erect posts, build fences and otherwise delineate the edges of their own space. A spiky cactus along the perimeter is probably designed to keep people out – a defence really, rather than a fence. Few barriers invite entry, although many are artfully conceived to embellish the appearance of the residence or attract attention.

Occasionally, highly inventive people have used the opportunity created by the need for a fence to build structures of unique character and creativity. Walls of bottles, shell decorations and walls topped with ornaments and sculptures tantalise and tease outsiders.

The wonderful flagon and saucer wall made by Don Salmon along the perimeter of the Millicent shell gardens ("all flagons donated...").

The Great Wall of Grotjahn

Amo's view of the world.

Arno Grotjahn has cemented his place in history by building vast walls of discarded objects on either side of his house.

Winton is a town in the arid area of far western Queensland, past Longreach and close to the opal fields. Arno Grotjahn's success in finding these beautiful stones at Opalton has made him one of Winton's best known characters, but his notoriety is increasing.

The town of Winton has a secure place in Australian history already – Qantas was formed at Winton in November 1920, and "Waltzing Matilda" was first sung in public in the bar of the North Gregory Hotel – but Arno Grotjahn is determined that every aspect of Winton's history will be thoroughly fixed for all time in his wall.

The walls reach two metres high and each extends for at least 70 metres. In them Grotjahn has displayed the rejected domestic, industrial, agricultural and mining paraphernalia of society. Equipment, machines and spare parts have been collected or donated and

resurrected, then finally appear with numerous rocks embedded in cement. One of Arno Grotjahn's ancestors fought alongside Peter Lalor at the Eureka Stockade, so the focal point of the array is a splendid declaration of independence, the blue and white Eureka flag surmounted here by a

version of the Aboriginal flag. The combined design is Arno's rebellious suggestion for Australia's new flag.

Sitting on top of the wall, silhouetted against the sky, are a sewing machine, miners' pit helmets, rock drills, bits, ventilator fans, car engines, an old typewriter, lawn mowers and an array of machinery that only a veteran engineer could identify. Circular wheels, metal cogs and wheels from huge abandoned tractors, cranes and trucks provide circular peepholes and a repetitive design element along the wall's full facade. In one alcove an Aboriginal figure surveys the street, frozen in time with his feet buried in cement.

Arno Grotjahn was born in 1930 in Bremen, Germany, and spent his youth as a merchant seaman travelling the world before emigrating to Australia with his wife Rita. The details of Grotjahn's early life at sea involve much mayhem.

There's a lot of drama, more than you think. I spent four years in the French Foreign Legion. I was in nearly every gaol in the world, but not in Australia. I didn't pinch anything – but if you jump the ship in a country, after a couple of days they get you. You are an alien, you've got no passport, nothing, so they put you in gaol.

It was during a nine month stay in Rome that Arno was inspired to build a wall later in his life. In 1947 Arno was sleeping in the hills outside Rome.

I used to sleep where the old Emperor lived. He left everything as it was, rocks falling in, even the old bedroom. You can still see the saunas, and the mosaics and the names like Tiberius, Claudius. Anyhow, I used to sleep there. In those

Arno Grotjahn's great wall of history. His rebellious suggestion for a new Australian flag celebrates Aboriginal pride and the great Eureka Stockade.

Examples of many past domestic and industrial inventions have been cemented in history.

OPPOSITE: A peep inside the Grotjahn wall shows materials for new walls awaiting resurrection.

days, you couldn't get work. I would go to the Vatican every three or four days to give me $5. There was a wall coming down the hills, it was 80 kilometres or maybe 90 and it had a sort of half arch with a pipe that brings water down from the mountains. That thing is 2000 years old. I thought I'd like to build something like that. That's how the idea started with my wall.

Arno Grotjahn is deeply contemplative, the result of spending large amounts of time alone in his small caravan out on the diggings. He can also pinpoint the origin of his fascination with opals that eventually led him to settle in Australia.

I started to dream when I was six or seven years of age. I always wondered what the place was in that dream. Millions of black pebbles, then sandstone. I always thought it was the moon or another planet or somewhere. That was one of the reasons why I always jumped ship – looking for that place – and ended up in gaol. Then we came to Australia and settled in Brisbane. One day on a German fishing boat a man opened a box and there were the opals. "Where did you get them?" I said, and he told me.

To Arno, the wall is special, even profound. He is reinstating the things others call rubbish to their rightful place as art.

It's a wall of history. It is incredible what's in there. There's a French typewriter. There is every artistic thing made. It is like the Mona Lisa – you can't copy that, and I'm not finished with it. I bought a little stove, beautiful. The people in the east, they won't appreciate things like that because it is all rubbish, rubbish, rubbish. For instance, they chucked the generator from the mine – those generators weighed nearly a tonne so I got it from the dump. It was already buried but I dug it out and they call me "Bloody stupid Arno. What's he doing there? He's digging." I had to get a forklift to bring it over to my place, but it's here now and it goes into the wall next year along with all those old shearing engines. I had to buy them and I went to the stations here and there, and I got everything, hand pieces and wheels.

The body of the wall is constructed of concrete and rocks that Arno brings to town from the mines in his Landcruiser's trailer. Many of the wall's rocks are mined from deep inside the earth.

I have put all sorts of rock and

boulders in the wall. Some are called moonstones. They are sort of round, from the size of a pebble to a car, and there's rocks from the mines. Come up and have a look, it's the most beautiful place in the world, out on the fields.

His introspective nature and vast experience of world religions during his early travels have given Arno a feeling of empathy with Aboriginal people and he occasionally comes across prehistoric evidence in the diggings that indicate an Aboriginal presence of many thousands of years.

I think those people were here 40–50,000 years ago. I think all life started here, going by my diggings – but I'm not an anthropologist. Those stone axes are down about one metre deep. They must have been here half a million years. In my mine there are also a lot of fossils. Tonnes of them, shells, fish, fossilised wood. They must have been really big trees on an old sea bed. I think the world must have been created here.

The antiquity of the Winton area is marked not only by its Aboriginal heritage, early European history and Grotjahn's wall, but by evidence of a dinosaur "stampede" 100 million years ago. Nearby, hundreds of dinosaur footprints have been frozen in the rock formed from mud that once edged an ancient lake.

In most climates the old metal objects in Arno Grotjahn's wall would rust and decompose quickly in the open, but at Winton (where it seldom rains) the wonderful wall of history will last longer, though perhaps not long enough to rival the Roman walls that inspired it or the ancient fossils beyond the town.

Fences, Defences and Wonderful Walls 83

Recycled Menageries

Kitsch and reworked junk have been the raw materials for art world constructions for most of the twentieth century, so it's not surprising that garden makers who employ these materials in their domestic displays are of riveting interest to post modernists. Cars stop, cameras click and viewers are bolted to the spot on beholding some of the more outlandish Aussie rebels in country towns who have decided to have a say, erect a visual treat or a message for the world to see.

The old Australian tradition of "making do", reinforced during the depression of the 1930s, gave "ordinary country people" many skills in reworking old tins (usually kerosene or petrol), and mending, screwing, bolting, or recycling any discarded item to a new and good use. Nothing was ever wasted or thrown out, so that sheds frequently housed endless items waiting for their owners to "get on to it".

Sometimes the discarded items of industry are still gathered by creative individuals who see a new use for them as the raw material for sculptures of their own design. These eclectic handymen (and some women) use farming, industrial and domestic rubbish and old machinery to create front yards where their characters are on the march, seldom hampered by trees, shrubs and foliage.

The garden gateway to Beau Hancock's world in a quiet valley in northern New South Wales. Old tools once used on his father's dairy farm are wired and welded into place.

Dungog Diorama – 4 U 2 C

Oliver Arthur Hancock and his wife Betty live among their jovial man-made companions on a sloping garden hillside just outside Dungog, on the New South Wales Central Coast.

Their companions were mainly constructed by Oliver ("Beau" or "Bowie" after the bowie knife he wore for 20 years) and painted by Betty.

The garden is a wild array of characters – tin, rubber, wood and cement. A few shrubs and trees survive but the paddock in front of the house is now largely used as a gallery for Beau's sculpture as well as displays of very old cement garden statues which he bought at various times during his travels.

Tour buses regularly stop in Fosterton Road, outside the Hancocks', to see the most famous menagerie in town. Three gates greet visitors on arrival, a special feature of this joyous if chaotic array of folk art: a brightly painted yellow and red turnstile, a wagon wheel gate, and the garden tools gate – a wide driveway entrance. On this gate the old farming and workshop tools Beau inherited from his dairy-farming father are welded fast or wired into place, then painted.

Beau is by his own admission "a bit of a wag", so the ferocious array of characters up front appear to jump out at the viewer, bare their teeth or say "Grrr" in mock threat – particularly the black pig sculpture and the "robot man".

Several sharks, their teeth gleaming as they lie low in the long grass staring ahead, seem to stalk the other inhabitants. Betty painted them all with sharp teeth and beady eyes so they would look suitably ferocious – "the hardest job of all". Beau made the sharks from things he found in the hills near Gresford.

The sharks were made from belly tanks for aeroplanes. That's what they used to put petrol in for the planes and when they finished, they just dumped them out in the bush, so that's when I got the idea to make a shark.

Beau (or Bowie) Hancock and friends.

LEFT: "Robot Man" was resurrected from a car's gas cylinder left in the Gresford dump.

OPPOSITE: Beau Hancock's amazing installation of recycled machinery, fairground paraphernalia and figures at Dungog.

Betty Hancock has enjoyed working with Beau on the garden. Most of the figures were bought in garden shops, from second-hand dealers, or from deceased estates. On a trip to town when a new "white boy" was to be purchased, Betty always felt mounting excitement.

I suppose it was because I painted them all, you see. You'd get them raw, although his favourites are very old indeed, probably 100 years old – they're those four white boys near the house, not the black one, you can get them, but not the others. They're very special. I work out the colours as I go along. I just paint a rock or put one colour on, see how it looks and then decide the next one. But the weather has to be right for painting, it can't be too hot or too cold.

The Hancocks' robot man, who has a friendlier face, was made from objects resurrected from the Gresford dump.

Yes, that's what that's made of – a gas producer that they used to have on cars years ago. It was put together with screws, nuts and bolts, wire, you name it, it all went in – everything from around the place.

In a continuation of the country "making do" tradition, the fierce pig guardian is made of recycled kerosene tins. Beau conceived it as a pig, but Betty, who took over the painting, had other thoughts.

He calls it the pig, I call it the dog because of the teeth in front of it – ever see a pig like that? Some people think it's the letterbox but that's just a little blue ordinary one – about the only thing around here that's sensible.

Beau Hancock was born in Newcastle, one of three brothers and three sisters. His

Ferociously-toothed sharks lurk in the grass. "The sharks were made from belly tanks from aeroplanes...they just dumped them out in the bush."

father was a farmer and although Beau began school at Gresford the family moved around the country so he changed schools often. He left school young, eager to see life away from home, and by 17 he had joined the circus. He was different from his brothers and sisters –"none of the others had the rambling in them".

Beau found his niche among the colourful cavalcade of characters that were drawn to circus life. According to Betty, Beau is still "a peacock" at the age of 66 and she points out a nesting pair of real peacocks down the back behind the house, the male a symbol of his "flash" owner as he spreads his colourful plumage and struts the estate.

Although Beau's main circus work was putting up the tents, driving in the stakes with the big wooden maul, he also worked as general labourer and cleaned up. He learned a few tricks along the way, especially with horses, and soon this became his livelihood.

He performed trick riding and also had a stretch boxing with "Jimmy Sharman's Boxing Troupe" among the sideshows. Members of the public were invited to go a round with him: "Step right up ladies and gentlemen – try your luck, test your strength and skill, with Bowie Hancock, come and have a look at the local boys."

Over the next 20 years Beau became a famous name in New South Wales country towns. A skilled rider, he worked the rodeos, riding wild bulls. With his first

OPPOSITE: Garden sculpture constructed from circular and crosscut saws, a calley axe and the maul Beau once used to hammer in circus tent pegs.

wife and child to support, skill and strength were his main means of earning a living.

But life changes, and Beau finally decided to "stop in one place", so he became a truck driver for the Dungog Shire Council and began his collection of cement figures. He had known his second wife, Betty, during his roving days and she was impressed with Beau's style.

Oh yes, I knew him. He used to travel in the rodeos, to Dubbo, Wellington and right around. It didn't matter where you went, you'd see him. He used to ride bikes in his young days, yes, but he gave them away. Then he used to have all the high society cars that you could mention. The last one was a Cobra, he also had a yellow GT – talk about flash! I just met him then, when I was a barmaid in the Goulburn Hotel.

Beau and Betty have now lived at their current house for about 10 years and Beau has retired from Council truck driving, a veteran of "30 years or more".

A number of works in Beau's garden have been made from pieces of machinery, old tractor parts and other cogs and wheels. One interesting assemblage combines circular saw, crosscut saw, a calley axe (suitably labelled as such) and the big wooden hammer called a maul used for hammering tent posts. Elsewhere an empty circular aviary sits as though the giant wire skeleton of a hot air balloon had just landed on the paddock. A cement policeman, inherited from a friend who made it, hides behind perpendicular stalks of cactus. His traffic sign says STOP to intending visitors, although from the house its other face, GO, allows the occupants to leave. Cut-up car tyres formed into goannas climb a telegraph pole which has

LEFT: The industry of Beau Hancock's dairy cow is admired by all as she labours up the paddock pulling her load of milk cans. Her horns are handlebars and her body is made from "factory" cans.

RIGHT: A nomadic "family" in Beau Hancock's garden wonder at the invasion of their land.

been brightly painted in red, white and blue and suitably labelled DANGER. At the side of the paddock, labouring up towards the gate, is one of Beau's most elaborate creations – a cow pulling a cart of milk cans. The cow itself has been constructed from milk cans or "factory cans" as they are known and its horns are a set of old bicycle handlebars. This piece is partly made to express Beau's nostalgia for his father's early days as a dairy farmer.

The Australian flag flies proudly above a handmade tin Australian coat of arms. Surmounted with a crown and including the kangaroo and emu, this fine piece greets visitors front-on within the display. A moon and a sun are added simply for effect and have no special meaning. Australian coats of arms also feature in the formidable array of cement figurines scattered over the property, along with kangaroos sitting motionless, as though paused momentarily in astonishment. Though at first glance it seems chaotic, thought and care have been used in the placement of objects. A group of Aboriginal figures stands with their backs to the viewer looking out over the countryside – perhaps thinking about these man-made changes to their natural environment. Santa Claus and his reindeer were previously strung between two jacarandas but the fastening broke and they now sit on the grass. Once a locked gate protected the Hancocks' property from intruders. The local policeman now suffices as a deterrent. Beau and Betty are delighted, however, with the visitors who come simply to look and admire, particularly the tourist buses.

Our kids thought the garden was beautiful and I'm glad that visitors come to see it, and many take photographs. We've got a sign out the front, did you see that? 4 U 2 C – glad we've got that sorted out.

Beau's decorative appearance marks him out from others in the town. Most locals know of his garden and either admire and like him and it, or don't say – his personal world is certainly unique in the district.

The rest are just ordinary places, ordinary workers around the town, some on the Water Board or the Council. There's very few, well, there's none like this garden, you can say that again.

JEPARIT JUNK SCULPTURES

Driving through Jeparit in western Victoria, a weatherboard house of particular interest erupts into view. Planes have crashed in the front garden, a silver mechanical man with a gun faces the enemy alone and the rear end of a scud missile is all that is visible of a direct Iraqi hit on the roof.

A crazy array of signage seems designed to bamboozle visitors who might be tricked into thinking the house was the local tourist information bureau.

This is the "garden" (or rather front yard) of Peter Kelm who, when the family farm had to be sold, moved into the nearby town of Jeparit taking his sculptural inventions and wayward aviation ideas with him. He chose a prominent house "with a street light out the front" to deter thieves and so far nothing has gone.

In the height of Victoria's rural recession Peter Kelm took to the paddock with a vengeance to make his first "quirky garden", best seen from the air.

In 1986, when I was back on the farm, I did a big write up about Bob Hawke; I used a tractor and a scarifier on two paddocks on the farm. One of them was "Hawk feathers his own nest and shits in ours", and alongside that was "Cut field taxes" and on the bottom I had "Fair go". And I made a figure of a windmill with the words "I support rural Victoria" and that went all over the place, Mike Willesee and quite a few news teams came down. Mostly everybody saw it. I got all my clippings and everything on it. I heard a little rumour the flying club in Nhill have got a good picture of it, I've never seen it. I didn't have an E on the end of his name, HAWK, until the newspapers said they wanted me to put the E on the end, so it all worked out.

The most complex sculpture in the Jeparit array is of a plough, horses and mechanical farmer, all made from junk – a prominent sign warns "Beware Jeparit Tip Monster". The plough was made by Peter Kelm's grandfather and Peter identifies strongly with the work calling it "the ex-cocky, that's me!"

The plough in the garden, well, my grandfather built that for the garden around the house on the farm. His name was Adolf Kelm. They came from near Germany, but he moved to Germany to find work and then from there he came to Australia. The plough has been in the Kelm family for a long time. Well, when I left the farm instead of selling it, I

When the recession forced Peter Kelm off his farm he turned his house into a museum in defence of the rural underdog. Ned Kelly and a hungry croc guard the front lawn from the government; Bob Hawke has already had a mauling; and a scud missile "meant for Canberra" has gone astray on the roof.

thought, I'll keep it, and I'll have it out the front. Then I made an extra figure out there and the two skinny horses, well they're supposed to be horses, whatever they are. That's all made out of my mind.

Most pieces are made out of "scrap" – discarded agricultural metal objects collected from the farms around the country nearby and the tip.

Most of it comes from other people's farms. They say "go for it". I'm doing them a good turn getting it off their farms – and making something out of nothing.

Most constructions have been made by welding the pieces together.

Since I was a kid, I sort of liked making things, sketching, things like that. I lived on the farm for a long time, 38 years. My dad bought a welder and I started making things. I was self-taught to use a welder and I was making these sculptures. When we were on the farm our relatives used to come and visit and see my stuff – the ones I've got out the front now, more or less. The farm was 10 miles out towards Horsham. We had sheep and pigs, cattle for milking, and wheat and barley. My grandfathers cleared the country for themselves. Goes back a long way. So that's where I started, on the farm. I've been in Jeparit for six years now. I just like to show people my work and that's why I've got things out the front.

The figure with the gun is Ned Kelly, the most infamous Victorian rural underdog hero of all.

That one is Ned Kelly, a bloke in Victoria – I put a shotgun in his hand just for the hell of it.

According to Peter Kelm, the "scud" missile on the roof was meant for Canberra politicians – but fell short.

One of Peter Kelm's welded sculptures greets the postman.

I heard all this Iraqi goings-on and the ministers were not doing too good, arguments. So I made a little story about this one – the Iraqis sent this rocket to Canberra for some unknown reason, but it missed and got me instead. Everybody who's seen it reckons it's a beauty. Meant for Canberra, but got me instead.

Another lost UFO sits behind a small row of ingenious model buildings at the side fence, called the "ghost town". A cut-out metal kangaroo and a giant wooden crocodile sculpture are the only wildlife: the crocodile, another example of Peter's fury at political targets, has just demolished the former prime minister – only a leg protrudes from its mouth.

Although unemployed since leaving the farm, Peter Kelm now occupies his time fully on volunteer work with the Jeparit Fire Brigade and maintaining machinery for the local "Primary Museum", as well as making garden folk art.

My garden's a bit different. Some people are quite jealous, they come up and say "What a heap of junk you got there". I say – you're just jealous you can't do it, that's all it is. I do get a lot of tourists, busloads, heaps.

Memorials to country pubs he has known line Peter Kelm's side fence.

Suitably Attyred

Romantic retreads are worked into garden fantasies of wild swan planters and arboreal reptiles.

Taming Nature

The ancient custom of trimming nature into shape produced the parterre, knot and maze gardens of Europe. This example is in Kingston, South Australia.

*T*rimming, teasing, torturing or simply tying Mother Nature in a knot is a folly once reserved for the grand estate gardens of Europe. But, just as smaller privet shoots colonise all corners of the garden, topiary fun has spread to the suburbs and country towns.

Hundreds of gardening books have told their readers that cypress pines, privet, box, yew and similar trees can be pruned to create dramatic shapes in the garden. With the use of a simple pair of garden shears, these trees have formed the basis of mazes, parterres and knot gardens made in the topiary technique.

Today they can be found in centuries-old castles, manors and cottages throughout Europe and England. Australia is new to the art of torturing nature in such neat formality, yet topiary gardens include many classic examples and also some singularly inventive designs.

THE EASTER ISLAND MAN

Cecil and Judy Bolton's topiary Easter Island Man stopped the traffic in Fairy Meadow, New South Wales, for a decade.

The cypress pine was already growing on the corner of the front of the house when the Boltons moved in, so Cec set to work. He had been inspired by the writings of Thor Heyerdahl, particularly *Kon-Tiki* which he read while sailing the seas in the navy. He spent many long nights gazing at the stars thinking of navigators from past centuries and developed a serious interest in astronomy. Before buying his house in Fairy Meadow, he had seen many illustrations of the Easter Island figures and thought deeply about Heyerdahl's theories. The idea that they were positioned in relation to the stars impressed him.

I thought if I could just make an Easter Island shape...so I chopped the eyes in and put a bit of a grin on him and then it was easy. I just had to cut it

"One look at the hedge and I could see the Old Man emerging so I set to work with the hedge cutters."

back more or less until the tree looked the right shape.

It has always stuck in mind, things like that. They're so old – those big heads just looking out to sea, those eyes looking out. Some sort of guardian. Why were they such a funny looking shape?

It was just a sudden inspiration to do something different...create public interest and get people thinking.

Today the old Easter Island Man no longer guards the Bolton's house. The Boltons say he might have been poisoned by someone in the street, others think Cec Bolton himself might have got too adventurous with the clippers. The suspicious circumstances of the Old Man's demise finished a remarkable career for the Easter Island Man whose role as guardian of the house is now taken by the family's small dog, suitably named Sirius.

Beside the "Enter at your own risk" and "Beware of the dog" signs, a new garden is emerging – almost equally odd, a higgledy-piggledy collection of shrine-like ornamentation including circlets of scallop shells, a lobster and various cacti. A spiky pandanus-looking plant has had its trunk literally tied into a knot by Cec, additional evidence of his tendency to thoroughly tame nature and perhaps a homage to more traditional knot gardens of the past.

MAREEBA MENAGERIE

The local Mareeba Council is unperturbed by the traffic hazard Tony D'Addona's gardening efforts have produced and recommend the garden to tourists and gardening enthusiasts as a notable example of unusual horticulture in the district.

"That lady, she sits on the chair...she's got her hands up and she says 'hello' to the people and waves to their car."

As you leave the coral cays of the tropical coast of Cairns in far north Queensland, head up the mountain road through the densely forested town of Kuranda and go out towards Mareeba and the tablelands, the highway turns past the solid brick house of Tony D'Addona and his hedges of topiary animals. A female figure sits on a chair on top of a bush, waving or beckoning to motorists who stop and stare.

Tony D'Addona was only 21 when he emigrated to Australia from the countryside near Naples, Italy. After stopping in Brisbane for several months and working with the gas company, he began seasonal work cutting sugar cane in the Mossman area. At that time it was all cut by hand and he remembers the period of hard work.

That's what I did for three years. When I finished with the sugar cane I came to Mareeba for the tobacco

On special days Tony D'Addona decorates his creatures with floral eyes.

season, then went to Victoria to pick some fruit, then came up here. That was too far away up and down. Enough. I stopped. I never went back. I found a job here as a builder and I stayed.

Tony D'Addona and his wife Assunta have been married for 23 years and have one daughter. They've spent their lives working in the district. D'Addona recently retired at the age of 61, not surprisingly due to a sore muscle in the back. His bad back has limited the creative genius of his gardening, but new developments are still possible as he eyes the municipal rose gardens opposite, "I'm planning a few shoots there", or offers to help friends establish suitable plants.

Horticultural details are not important to Tony D'Addona, it's the image that begins to emerge from the bush, the amusement it brings him and the reward of fame and notoriety.

To tell you the truth I tried to find the name out of the bushes. A friend of mine gave it to me, it's like the hedge bush.

D'Addona explains the many characters in his green menagerie.

I got kangaroo, a wolf dog who feeds the twins, Romulo and Remo, another lady on a chair, another little horse and a big one. A chooky, a duck, now a little elephant and that's all. That lady, she sits on the chair. First of all I make the round tree on the bottom, then the chair on top, then her sitting there. She hasn't got a name but she should really.

Well, it started a long time ago. I went to my friend's place one time and he did one plant with the little thing on the top like a horse or dog or something like that. I thought this would be good in my place, right in the middle of the road. It could look nice. as people pass by. So I tell him, when you prune it, you keep me a few shoots I want to plant. But when I start, I start wrong, you see, I let it go and

Retired farmer Tony D'Addona tends his animals along the Mareeba Highway.

I didn't know what to do with it. But after I chop it off and I make all the round bush on the front and after I start, I see a shoot coming up and I start thinking on the top of this one, we can put some other thing on. Looks better. So I start with a goat and after a kangaroo, after a lady on the chair, after I leave a little bit there to grow, like the lady sit on the chair. And another little horse on the other side and little kangaroo and there was a little horse with a rider on it.

There have been a few mishaps with Tony's privet garden due to vandals who come to Mareeba at rodeo time.

Some stupid idiots, they pass here and they chop all the heads off, one behind the other. In the morning I was so angry I was green, like the grass.

Repairs take time as the shoots have to appear, grow and then be clipped

again, hopefully into a suitable form; this might explain some of the more unusual anatomical features of the animals in the D'Addona garden. The horse on the nature strip and his companions are all travelling in the same direction as the traffic, but the horse is missing an important part: "Yes, I know he's got to have the wee wee. I tried but it's hard for shoots to grow down." Tony D'Addona explains other anomalies with a twinkle in his eye.

One Aussie said to me, "The lady, she get too fat." I say, "Yes mate, she's a dago woman with a big bum".

Most of Tony D'Addona's topiary is achieved simply by clipping and shaping the form. However the newest addition, the elephant, has required some reinforcement.

With the elephant I put a piece of

Encourage one shoot on top of the privet and amazing things may emerge, like the duck in the Parlapiano vineyard at Mareeba.

I never give them any name yet. Just the front of the house, no name. I just did it to have something to do on the weekend. Now even the people from Mareeba stop and look and now they've got used to it. Even the tourist buses, stop and take a photo, a movie.

Tony D'Addona is a good friend of Tony Parlapiano, another Mareeba resident. The two men obviously spend a lot of time in the garden behind the Parlapiano house where a hedge of animals guards a row of prickly pear bushes and a small vineyard.

D'Addona's dog, goat, "or whatever you like". If the shoots grow waywardly, the animal's features change so Tony D'Addona is happy for viewers to interpret the result themselves.

wire there because, you know the long nose he got, I am trying to turn it around and bring it up. So I put a piece of wire in there and just tied it up with a piece of string for a while and then when they get the form, they just stay there, you see.

ANIMALS ON PARADE

A giant swan looms over a blue agapanthus border of a small garden in Unanderra, a suburb outside Port Kembla, New South Wales. The swan calls for the garden to be noticed as she bends to nuzzle her breast feathers with her beak – and it is.

This is the garden of Daphne Naylor who lives in Rose Parade. The thought of daphne and roses conjures up scented arbours of delicate English plants. Mrs Naylor's garden does indeed have beautiful flowers all around the yard, day lilies, hydrangeas, canna lilies, many different bulbs, even roses – but it's not the flowers that have given her fame. It's the parade of animals she has carved from privet bushes through the garden.

Mrs Naylor originally came from Brewarrina in the far west of New South Wales: "I'm a true blue Aussie from Bre." After a period in Orange, she and her husband moved to Unanderra, where they stayed for about 42 years while Mr Naylor worked as a rigger for the Australian Iron and Steelworks Company in Port Kembla.

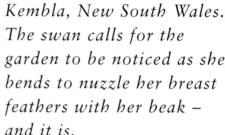
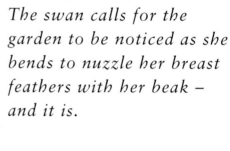

LEFT: Daphne Naylor delicately prunes the "basket of ivy" she trained over the skeleton of a deceased lemon pine.

RIGHT: Like a giant inflated mascot, Daphne Naylor's cypress swan dominates her front garden.

He was very strong but he had a very bad heart which we never knew until he became real ill. That's what killed him. He died 11 years ago last month. The garden gave me something to occupy the mind I suppose.

Mrs Naylor's husband apparently had little interest in the garden, so she became "the home labourer" growing vegetables, putting down pavers and making a greenhouse. When he died, she began her topiary fantasies. The inspiration for these is clear – the pleasure it gives her grandchildren and the comments she receives from passers-by.

I never learned how to do it. I just thought I'd have a go for myself. I started with the swan and that was by accident. I cut down a big pine tree which was beginning to hit the electric wires and then it sort of branched out everywhere and I thought I'd tie one back as a tail and one for the head and let it grow and so I shaped it from then on. Then there were another couple of pines, one was a lemon pine, a square one with a round ball on it and a sort of basket on top. In the meantime that has died and I have put wire all over it and covered it with ivy.

I've also got a lot of privet animals – a kangaroo out of privet hedge and an emu. The kangaroo is about 5 feet, I suppose, up to the head, but the emu's only about 3 feet. They all came out of my mind. With the kangaroo I just grew a row of hedges to start, left the top end grow small and kept cutting the bottom end for the tail. I kept them short and didn't let them grow.

Then my little grandkiddies, I have five grandkids, they used to say

An example of indigenous fauna in Mrs Naylor's garden.

"Grandma, make an elephant" and I said "I'll give you the four trees and you start it." So my little grandson grew the four trees and from then on I sort of clipped it into shape for him. So now we've got an elephant. I've made quite a few in the last few years. I've also got a bird. I had in mind a dove, but at the moment it looks more like a turkey! The grandkids would always say "Make another one Grandma". And I'd think what could we make. And I'd say "What about a giraffe? What about a kangaroo?" And they'd say "Yes!"

The garden animals have taken the place of live pets. A lot of children pass Mrs Naylor's house and ask to see the animals and this contact gives her great pleasure. Mrs Naylor was nonplussed when one neighbour christened the elephant Sylvia (after herself) so she is presently thinking of other names for her creations before their identities are similarly usurped by onlookers.

A local artist took some photographs of my garden and put one in an exhibition. They sent me an invitation from the Council and had a champagne night and I saw it. They had slides of different places from all around the area and it was a very good turnout. Everyone was there and proud of their own.

Since then Mrs Naylor has made many more animals and people passing offer comments and praise. She is bemused by some remarks.

Even men, they walk past and one man said "Your garden is very nice, I walk by every day and admire it". I don't even know the man but he says hello as he passes. You wouldn't think men would be bothered to take notice of things, but I suppose some men have interests in gardens too – some do, some don't.

Tied in a Knot

Some gardeners like Christine Doyle in Kingston, South Australia prefer to emulate classic knot gardens in both design and planting.

When the vacant block next door was for sale ten years ago, the Doyles purchased it. Putting lawn there would have meant more mowing, so as keen gardeners and herbalists a knot garden was the best solution.

Knot gardens date back to the early seventeenth century. They evolved from medieval herb and kitchen gardens and generally consisted of low lying interlocking designs that later developed into the puzzles that inspired mazes.

Mrs Doyle's garden has santolina, rosemary, box, white thyme and other cottage garden plants. The edges are planted with roses. Mrs Doyle and her father established the garden and maintain it with shears and electric hedge cutters. The ankle-high patterns they created are reminiscent of Celtic designs or the low relief patterning on long-abandoned tombs and gravestones in Cornwall, Wales and the islands off the coast of Scotland.

The Doyles' Kingston knot garden.

Wind and Water Wonders

Decorative weather vanes and whirligigs are known in numerous countries, where their presence celebrates the movement and power of the wind. Whirligigs are an old English tradition derived from toys that were whirled, twirled or spun around. Many of these old toys had four arms like windmill sails and whirled when they moved through the air. Strategically placed whirligigs revolve continually, whirling and twirling in the sky.

Water features are also common to many gardens, from the lily lagoons of the grand estates and fountains of the rich to a simple fish pond beneath the ferns adorned with gnome fishermen, frogs or cement pelicans. For most, the sound of water trickling in a beautiful garden evokes peaceful thoughts. Quiet places of nature combined with the sound or reflections of water seem to bring a sense of contentment, perhaps harking back to a harsher human existence centuries before, when finding water on long journeys or bringing it from the well was an arduous task.

To some, however, the importance of these elements is so profound their entire garden has been turned into a celebration of these qualities.

This classic homage to the essential elements of wind and water is a front lawn feature of the residence of Ellen and Neville Smith at Wyong, New South Wales.

WHIRLIGIG WONDERS

Martin Humphreys' garden whirligigs are tall windmills of animated characters who perform when the wind propels their intricate mechanisms. Each is a carved wooden "character" from folklore village life.

OPPOSITE: The neighbours' view of Martin Humphreys' back yard.

The penny-farthing rider pedals continuously on a 30 metre high stand. On an average windy day he would cycle from Bendigo to Melbourne and back.

Born on a small farm in Wales, Humphreys left it as a teenager and became a fitter, then later joined a travelling fair where he assembled rides and equipment. The colour and vibrancy of his experiences at the fairground were recreated in his garden of whirligigs at Long Gully, a few kilometres out of Bendigo. Although he has now moved to another property, his passion for whirligigs continues unabated and he is busy establishing a new whirligig garden.

All the whirligigs are painted brightly in primary colours, the characters move animatedly, high against the bright blue sky. One of the most commonly made whirligig figures is a woman drawing water from the well, once a daily chore. Other repetitive village activities like washing clothes, churning butter and chopping wood are also part of whirligig tradition. One of Martin

The ferris wheel – a
celebration of Humphreys'
fairground youth.

Humphreys' creations, "the old woman chasing the pig" has caused some local comment.

I've been told that Australian women don't chase pigs, but I'm sure they do. My mum certainly does, in fact it's quite a common activity in Wales.

He has a rotating Ferris wheel, a cuckoo clock and also a wonderful penny-farthing rider who pedals madly as the breeze catches the windmill blades of the big wheel. This whirligig is over two metres tall and stands on top of a seven metre tower.

I've calculated that if he was travelling down the Calder Highway, he would cycle from Bendigo to Melbourne and back on an average windy day, or even further on a very windy day.

Making whirligigs is a delicate and sometimes frustrating process. Most of Martin's materials come from the tip. Whirligigs must have bearings on the various joints and all the moving parts must be well oiled in order to turn freely. Martin is meticulous in ensuring that the whirligigs are well-balanced or they will not move.

Like other windmill and whirligig fanciers, a windy day fills Martin Humphreys with pleasure as he watches his "little folk" come to life. He loves the idea that the energy of the wind, which costs nothing and does not damage the environment, can be so easily harnessed. However, he is sometimes forced to curse the wind. After a heavy storm, the whirligigs are in disarray – pieces might be tangled or missing and mechanisms damaged from the sheer force of the gale.

OPPOSITE: Whirligig titled "Old woman chasing a pig", a theme from English village life.

WINDY DAY WINDMILL GARDEN

At Katoomba in the Blue Mountains of New South Wales, Ivan Romanov has filled his yard with a garden that whirls, hums and sings on every windy day.

Ivan Romanov's back garden whirls and sings on every windy day reminding him of the carriage wheels for Russian caravans he made with his father long ago.

It is a joy for Ivan Romanov to look out his door and see his moving sculptures – windmills fashioned from his imagination from numerous pieces of recycled junk.

Leichhardt Street heads down the mountain ridge from the Katoomba township. The houses are all small cottages. At first, Number 10 appears to be just like its neighbours until a huge paraphernalia of whirligigs on tall poles comes into view around the side. These reach into the sky, framing the blue mountain ridge in the distance, rattling and dancing like a miniature carnival on stilts. Fortunately for Ivan Romanov who has spent 20 years of his retirement making these marvellous contraptions, his next door neighbour and friend entirely approved of this undertaking and even helped.

My neighbour had one tonne Japanese truck. He tells me, "We going shopping to rubbish tip, behind hospital. You want going with me?" I going, he going. He was a very very big rubbish man.

The Romanov Windmill Garden consists of over 50 wind mobiles made from raw materials scavenged from the dump including old bicycle wheels, detergent bottles, paint tin lids, pie dishes, children's toys, miniature tennis racquets, tea trays, pizza trays, even airconditioning units.

On a very windy day, their flashing colours, the sound of the wind rattling the contraptions madly and the squeak and music of rods rotating on their bearings cause Ivan Romanov to smile in a reverie of pleasure, thinking of gypsy caravans, balalaika music and his eight decades of hard work.

My father was a farmer, he built horses' cars, troika, for working horses. He was a smart man, he knew everything. He was not in school one day, ever. He was a specialist. He built gypsy carts with steps and he built buggies. My father was not like capitalist, not much land. We were very

Recycled windmills co-exist with a lone flowering shrub, the spectacular red mountain waratah.

Marvels from the Katoomba tip soar again.

poor. East Siberia, near China, was empty, not too many people, unpopulated. So in 1915 he helped people going to emigrate. So they did. Not pay too much for train, cheap. He transferred them there, drive them from Kaukas to far east. I, a small boy, was with him 5 years. Far east empty, plenty land, wood, bush, deer.

I finished only village school, no more. In school I was not bad at mathematics. I counted very quick. My father had eight children, I was biggest.

When I was 12 or 13, I wanted balalaika. My father buy good balalaika, cost 3 roubles, must work 3 days. Father not want buy. I think he think I never play. He start make himself balalaika. He working, he made balalaika, but he make the stomach

In this metaphor for life's pitfalls, the woodcutter earnestly chops away at his own foundations.

behind, like violin, guitar, he make from tin, not timber. Nice melody. Russian compositions. Good music. In the village there's nothing, only we make farm, for music we must sing, not like now with TV.

I went to school there for four years, then finish, live with my father until Communist destruction 1929, 1930, I was 19 years old. My friend gave me a book, I read it good, from start to finish, Russian economic, politic, Lenin's book. I tell my father "We will be finished. Better we run away somewhere." My father say "I am working all my life, like donkey. Leave everything? Run away?" We travel somewhere, go to work, with horses. After 1929, finish. My father gets caught, he spoke against communism. They put him in prison, concentration camp, working. They keep him maybe four years, then out. I was son, communist government don't trust me. When I have time in Russian army, I was 20 or more 21, for national service, they sent me to special camp, for re-education.

After my father was freed, he ran away to China, to Manchuria. No-one heard from him again.

I go to railway working, carrying coal to firemen with wheelbarrow. After mining, I get to fish. I worked one season, one summer, catching herrings.

I went only once. Bad sea, vomit, so don't work any more. Then in communist organisation young man, he say "We want barber". I say "I am barber", but I am not barber. But I'm going to barber shop, I bought scissors and I'm cutting. Public baths, I'm barber. They say "Where you study?" I tell them "I study with my father, he was barber". "Where is your father?" "Dead!" "All right, you come tomorrow in office, young man." They don't know. I work as barber, better money, it's clean, warm and so on.

After the German occupation of Russia, Ivan Romanov was sent to work in a German transport company, first in Germany, then in Italy, where he met Rossina, his wife, who refers to him as "my smart professor".

The Romanovs emigrated to Australia in 1955 and settled in Sydney. By extraordinary thrift, Ivan managed to accumulate some money. "All the money in bank, in bank, in bank." He worked in Bondi Junction in a shoe factory but in his spare time privately cut hair for cash. When he retired, he and Rossina bought the house at Katoomba and at last he was free to begin his years of invention.

I like to be inventor but I start too late. In Russia I made for my mother potato scraper, scratch flour, scratch potato. From this mother make pudding, make milk. I like to be inventor – I have invented 50 windmills. I am happy when I look at them going around but I am always busy because they are breaking in the wind.

Out in the garden there are frequently sounds that cause Ivan consternation.

The wind blows down the kewpie doll mobile regularly. Even broken, with some adjustment she is erected again and her arms go around madly in the wind. Billy the goat watches dully over the back gate eyeing the struggling rare plants, beneath the aerial cacophony. A blossoming waratah tree, that special sacred flower of the mountains, had brought forth many splendid blooms on its well-nibbled branches. The mountain soil and climate are perfect for any flowering plants and shrubs. Lilac scents the Romanov drive and wild daisies rampage through the old stone walls. But plants hold no interest for Ivan Romanov. It's all Rossina can do to occasionally get him to help dig the vegetable garden, before he returns to his small workshop in the yard to make another windmill.

There are three kinds of windmill – two wing, four wing, six wing. I like to see them, I like to see the colour. It makes me happy. Beautiful! I like beautiful.

Among the tin and plastic sculptures are some of Ivan Romanov's more successful creations: the wood chopper, the policeman and the bird. The wood chopper, from old European folk art, chops away at the very structure he is standing on, while the policeman turns wildly on his pole waving furious directions to all the other whirling traffic of the garden.

Life has been exceptionally difficult for both Ivan and Rossina, but the garden has achieved a remarkable presence in the mountains and is known by all who appreciate a bit of fun and eccentricity in the rarefied mountain air.

Foil pizza trays catch the
sunlight like swirling
discuses.

WATER GARDEN

For decades, the garden of Germano Capaldo in one of the main streets of Adelaide aroused regular comment in the press whenever a new invention appeared.

The heading of an article in the *Advertiser* on Friday, 11 November 1977 read "Mr Germano Capaldo is not finished yet". This is true even 17 years later although the ivy is now rampant and the plants need tending.

On most days Germano Capaldo sits looking at pedestrians from behind the overgrown paraphernalia of the front yard that has been his obsession for 40 years. The little house now seems dwarfed by the city development which surrounds it, but the garden still draws attention with its cacophony of noisy moving parts, statuary, water wheels, fountains, squirting jets, masonry cats, dogs, elephants, a rocket on the roof, weather vanes and bird cages. Two huge windmills in the backyard garden pump water to the top of the house. This not only airconditions the house but on a good windy day the water flows on through different pipes and channels to the fountains and constructions in the front garden. The power of the water moves these in various ways to create an animated tableau.

Every item in this colourful array has been ingeniously conceived to give expression to water and wind power. Germano Capaldo has clearly had a hard life in which a reliable source of pure water has played an important role in his well-being. His conversation is full of comments about water, particularly the disaster of the Murray River. He blames everyone in New South Wales for the fact that there is no good water in the Murray River any more.

Everyone in New South Wales wash, sex, swim in river, nobody ever worry about South Australia. I never drink the water. I get rain water.

The inner-city wonderland in Adelaide where Germano Capaldo makes his own water from windmills and water wheels. Tiered towers and planters pay homage to other great Italian gardens.

Glance upwards and Germano Capaldo's rocket ship, weathervane and international clock fill the sky. "One day soon I will get up there and clean it for you - it is still telling the time."

During his early working life Germano Capaldo was a market gardener. His life story in his own words is "a big story", with worrying elements of tragedy, violence and loss about which he does not elaborate but which have made him a loner.

When I came to Australia in 1929 I made many houses, Mt Lofty, Uralla, Piccadilly, Virginia. The only real Australians are black fellows. When they were here and nobody else, water was on top of the ground, now you have to make a bore, because it is under.

They asked me what you do – I'm a market gardener. I send celery to Sydney and Melbourne, bleach it in crates. I never go to war. We collect the vegetables for military. I was naturalised two weeks before the war, but my brother was not so they locked him in a camp.

In the front garden Germano Capaldo has made a huge water clock and water wheels. The clock tells both overseas and local time. In an album full of decades of press reports of his garden, he also has postcards and snapshots of his overseas trip, particularly his visit to Italy. The Tivoli and Villa D'Este Roma Fountains take pride of place – the ultimate achievement emulated in Germano Capaldo's garden in theme if not in the same grand style.

Features of his garden include tyres stacked in tiers much like a wedding cake. The sizes range from huge grader and tractor tyres down to car tyres; all are used as planters. One set is suspended on a pedestal made of a metal drum with windows cut in the sides with tin snips. On the roof are two weathervanes: one a cone-shaped series of windsocks in red,

and the other, more bizarre, in the shape of a rocket.

A sunken tank in the back yard holds the water produced from his two windmills and pumps. The first bore sunk went down 30 metres – "nothing", the second bore descended only 10 metres before good water was located. There are two water taps. "This one is government water, this is my water", he says proudly. Germano Capaldo can not believe the ignorance of some visitors who ask him to demonstrate some of his elaborate cut tin vane-like constructions. He looks at them as though they are daft. "Water comes only in the wind."

On the right side of the front garden a cement bridge and lighthouse are surrounded with plants and statuary. Pan plays his pipes in the corner. On the left side of the garden a tiered succession of bowls descend from the roof like a series of rock pools. Shaped like rubbish bin lids, each pours its water into a larger fluted metal pool below. The edge of each pool is further decorated with concrete figurines of dinosaurs and fish.

On a windy day an elaborate web of tubes sprays water upwards to produce a full fountain effect from the dishes cascading from the roof. There are other windmills made of Coca-Cola cans that fly into wild action and clatter furiously in the wind.

The face of the huge international time clock is now opaque and the numbers are hardly visible but Germano Capaldo assures me that inside it is still telling the time of many cities of the world and is still a landmark in Adelaide. One day soon he will get up there and clean it so we can see it again.

Well-Planted

A foot in the
right garden, a
well-planted pot
or well-potted
plant.

Minimal Maintenance Gardens

Occasionally, inventive people are found who have devised a solution to the frustration of nature's capriciousness or to the boredom of the hard work required by plants and lawns. Their solutions have produced front yards that require minimal maintenance yet give expression to their owners' decorative ability.

Some follow Japanese tradition, with raked gravel, boulders or stones and minimal plant life. Australians either imitate the Japanese aesthetics, or erect more outlandish local prototypes with boulders, rocks, gravel, even tree stumps and petrified wood. In outback environments these thrive better than lawns and flowering shrubs.

One of the most common motivations for establishing unusual low maintenance gardens, apart from the creative fun it offers garden artists, is the determination which do away with that labour-intensive and time-wasting Australian pastime of mowing the front lawn. The continuous watering, feeding and mowing cycle has led a number of gardeners to simply remove the lawn altogether, replacing it in different ways. In one household in Medindie, South Australia, a spectacular result has been achieved by replacing the lawn with thousands of iridescent blue-green fragments of glass. The glass was collected over a long period and then tumbled to smooth the edges. It sparkles and gleams in the sun and looks particularly fresh and pretty after the rain. The owners were amazed at the immense interest it produced and although trespassers are deterred by the thought of cut feet, the bevelled edges are very smooth.

Pebbles, painted pathways and a Stonehenge of rocks and petrified wood are the solution to lack of water in outback Kalgoorlie.

OPPOSITE: The perfect solution to lawn mowing fatigue – a front lawn of glass. The fragments glisten in the rain and won't cut feet as they've been tumbled smooth.

THE ROCK GARDEN OF KINGAROY

Harry and Margaret Labudda's garden at Kingaroy in Queensland is more than a rockery: it could be a miniature mountain range, a model of the Bungle Bungles or Boulder City.

OPPOSITE: Harry Labudda ripped out his prize-winning garden and replaced it with the glowing colours of agate and jasper and the allure of petrified wood from a prehistoric forest only he knows.

The Labuddas have been collecting rocks all their lives; indeed when they first met, Margaret recalled, they each had little rock specimens in matchboxes.

When we met I showed him what I had and he showed me what he had. We were both interested in that type of thing.

Their interest has escalated over the years. The Labuddas' house and land now runs over two allotments and all available space is covered with rocks. It could be described as littered with rocks – but this would not be true, as each rock has been carefully placed according to its type and colour and then cemented in. Making the garden has been back-breaking work but the colours and forms of the rocks are interesting enough in themselves for Harry to justify replacing the living garden that preceded them.

The Labuddas' garden used to be somewhat ordinary. Situated around an historic museum display, it was pretty enough to warrant entry in the local garden competition. Indeed Harry won the competition in 1960. He recalls that, like the other winning gardeners of the district, he expected to be given his certificate and prize in the local hall by Mrs Bjelke-Petersen, wife of the former Queensland premier, and a prominent identity in Kingaroy, her home town. But as Harry says:

The ladies weren't happy. I wasn't in the Society [horticultural or garden].

That was before I had the rocks. It was all flowers and things. So they didn't hand it to me. They simply put a four guinea cheque in my mailbox.

Discouraged, Harry decided to pull all the garden up and start something new. He began by putting in cement paths and paving, taking out the offending lawn that reminded him of the years he had spent labouring over the grass at the local school where he was the groundsman for 19 years.

Everything I've done in my life, I try to cut out work and painting. I mowed the lawn at Kingaroy State School for 19 years and I didn't want to do it for the rest of my life. That's why I'm making a garden that won't need that type of work – although, mind you, I've got four and a half chains of footpath grass still to mow.

The colours in Harry's rocks are spectacular as Kingaroy is close to remarkable geological areas and the family have travelled to outlying outcrops all their lives. The first sight the Labuddas' had of rocks containing crystals, had them hooked. Friends who lived in the Windera area near Murgon and Wondai simply used them as decorative stones sitting around their pot plants but the Labuddas developed much grander ideas. They travelled to the area nearly every weekend for years until they had collected stones and rocks of all types – beautifully coloured agate and red jasper from

Windera and blue-green stone from Gympie. Some of the most unusual rock displays are actually petrified tree stumps, two of which guard the entrance to the Kingaroy property. These are obviously millions of years old. Harry Labudda talks of the excitement of finding them in an ancient forest on top of a range.

Oh, we go everywhere, up creeks, over ranges, following the ringbarkers' tracks. Sometimes we get stuck in trees and it's bloody hard work. I had to hire a big trailer for the two and a half tonnes stumps of petrified wood. You have to dig them out when they're still standing. They're still standing there today where the trees grew. That area used to be a lake bed and further out it was the ocean, but now it's on top of the range, pushed there millions of years ago. The whole ridge is covered with smooth rocks and I collect them all up so the school can sell them. The kids paint them as pet rocks and they made $150 out of the last lot I gave them.

Harry Labudda was born in Roma and brought up around Kingaroy. He worked in a range of different jobs in his youth – just about everything, he says – but in particular farm work and chipping peanuts. For a while the couple had a dairy farm from which they made enough

to buy a house in Kingaroy. As soon as the family could purchase an old car they set off to collect rocks. The garden still attracts a great deal of comment from tourists and visitors to Kingaroy, the peanut capital of Australia. The gardening program *Burke's Backyard* visited and Harry Labudda proudly recounts –

When Don Burke came here he said only three things: "I love it, I love it, I love it".

The former premier Joh Bjelke-Petersen accompanied Don Burke, thereby redeeming the family from the previous ignominy of the garden award being placed in the letterbox rather than handed to Mr Labudda.

Although designed as a minimal maintenance garden, the small rounded pebbles between the large rocks occasionally pose a problem, particularly when digging the soil to plant the few palms and shrubs the Labuddas allow. In addition, Harry has to cope with annoying leaves that get stuck in the cracks between the rocks and the cement.

The leaves are the big problem. They come from the park down the road and the neighbours' trees and I've got to rake them up or take them out by hand as they stick in the wall.

It is also hard to imagine that the garden has cut down on Harry's physical work in his retirement. The rocks have to be collected in the trailer and then placed in the garden with a winch, or manhandled into position with a crowbar and a big barrow. The very large ones require a big wallaby jack and Harry feels he might even need a crane for the large specimen of quartz he is contemplating erecting in the front garden. Petrol is also expensive: in the last year Harry spent $1,500 on the 50 trips he made into the bush. But the result is spectacular, a true rock museum to replace the former pioneer museum which Harry once kept. His sheds are still full of old sulkies and the first peanut thrasher in Kingaroy. There are even dinosaur footprints in stone kept in the garage.

I retired four years ago but I've never worked harder since.

Harry's rock work continues unabated; although his own land is almost full, he has started off new gardens for friends with what he calls "petrified mailboxes" and walls. To appreciate the garden's intense colour it needs rain which is a scarce commodity at Kingaroy – so a good hose-down often does instead.

THE PERPETUALLY BLOOMING GARDEN

Janet Ritchie owns an Edwardian mansion in the heart of cosmopolitan Melbourne.

Situated in Ackland Street, St Kilda, the old dark Hawthorn brick house is now four units. For the past nine years, Janet has cared for her young child, and managed the flats.

Her garden is a bright and safe haven in an area which has considerable social problems.

I began the garden really because I was angry. It was all dirt and rubble, and young street people would throw sharp things over the fence. I had a very young son and we needed somewhere safe to play. You couldn't grow lawn because of the big trees in the street, too much shade, so we put down the artificial turf, and it's really good – I can see everything and I just need to vacuum up the leaves every two weeks or so. I drilled holes in it for drainage so that the trees would be all right and that seems to prevent mould too.

The garden grew – it now has co-operative plastic flowering plants throughout, together with figurines and gnomes. The blooms never fail and the Melbourne frost is thwarted, so that Janet's little haven has a colourful year-round display.

The window boxes contain geraniums that never discolour; real and artificial ivy climbs the bricks – initially to hide a crack, now mended – and fake flowers glow with colour in boxes on the side fence. In summer Janet brings out impatiens, also minimal maintenance flowers that bloom for months, to add to the colours of this iridescent space.

My "ex" added the goldfish ponds, and I bought the gnomes and put the flowers and plants around – it's so green now and always nice. All that I've done has been to save having to do too much work – even the goldfish are hardy and live long – you just throw a pinch of fish food in every few days.

At one time, 60 gnomes lived in this front garden but most have been kidnapped; those that remain are rooted to the spot with cement.

People would come in and steal them, mostly at night. There's an idea around that it's OK – they need a new home. Sometimes I got a note left behind, "Your gnome has decided to move to a new garden". But I kept buying them.

This garden of artificial flowers and ornamental turf is maintained by vacuum cleaner rather than by lawn mower.

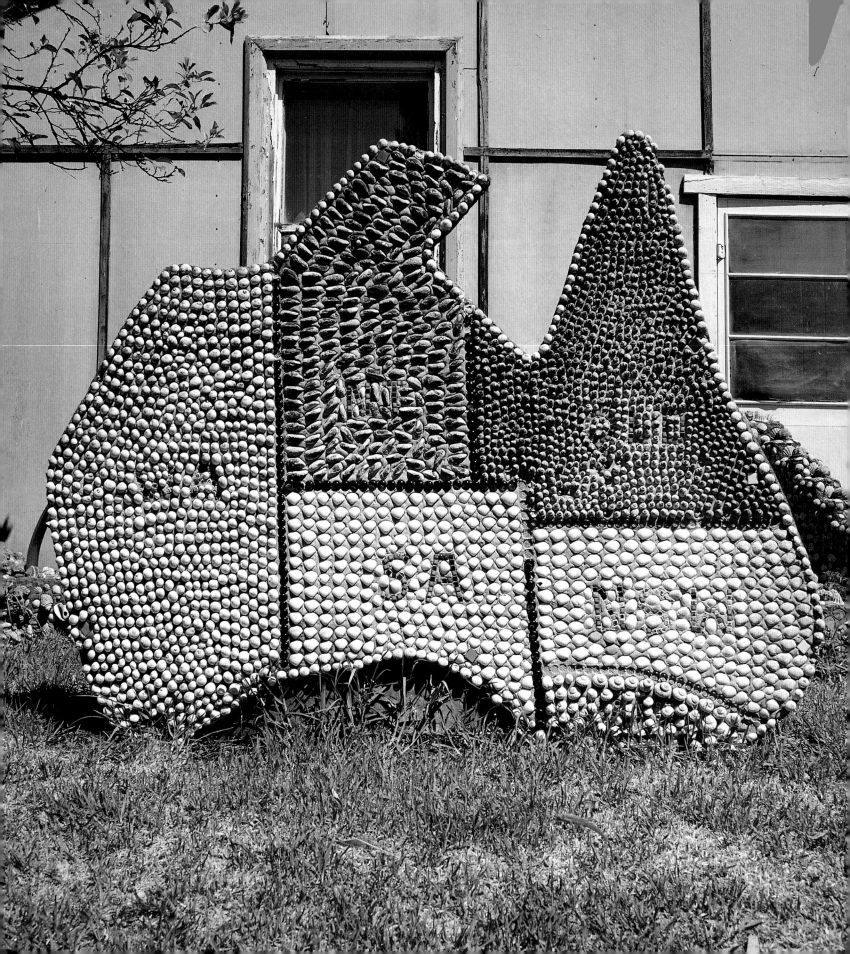

Australian Landmarks

The preparation, publicity, construction and finally official opening of some of Australia's major architectural and engineering feats have been known to fire the imagination of garden artists. They are often men who previously worked in the construction business as builders or labourers and who admire the power and image of "man's greatest achievements". Paying homage to the larger structures, they create miniature replicas in their own gardens both for the admiration of others and for their own satisfaction. Frequently the subjects are Australia's most famous sites – the ones seen on the postcards bought by countless tourists.

"My own Australia." The shell garden emblem of patriotism at Wolseley, South Australia.

CORRIMAL CONSTRUCTIONS

In Corrimal, former miner and builder Joe Harriman has constructed his own front garden homage to the three major Sydney Harbour tourist landmarks: the Bridge, Luna Park and the Opera House.

Corrimal is a small seaside community south of Wollongong. Its streets, built in a grid pattern to house the workers in the nearby colliery and steel works of Port Kembla and Wollongong, are home to a number of unusual gardens, many made by immigrants who came to Australia in the early part of this century to work in the industrial complex. Joe Harriman's father had been a coal miner in Durham, Northern England.

From the time he was 13, Joe Harriman was anxious to escape the rigours of poverty. Various schemes were offered to enable fit young men to emigrate to Australia, Canada or New Zealand and he urged the family to emigrate.

We came just like everybody else. We thought that the grass was greener elsewhere. I'd been a niggling boy at home before I brought all the family here. When I was about 12 years of age, I started niggling that we would have to

get out of the mining village and go to Canada, New Zealand or Australia, and of course the invitation was handed out to boys that were willing and if I could have got my mother and father to sign on the dotted line I could have left school at 13 years and 9 months, and

OPPOSITE: In his garden shed Joe Harriman pays homage to men's and women's hard physical labour through a display of the rural and industrial tools of the past.

Joe Harriman's cabbages and spuds have long since given way to his constructions celebrating great Australian engineering feats, buildings and places.

come to Australia, wouldn't cost a farthing. You were taken from your home, and in those days you'd be planted on a cocky's farm, 10/- a week, and must be able to milk and ride, that was the job. Dad used to say to me, "Pipe down, you'll break your mother's heart if you start any of that sort of caper. I'll promise we will all try to go together."

At last when the family arrived in Australia together in 1928 on the SS *Otranto*, Joe Harriman, his brothers and

his father worked as coal miners. Joe worked "with the horses in the mines for four years" between the ages of 14 and 18. The mining life in those days was extraordinarily harsh.

This wasn't in the Dark Ages, this was in my time, the 1914 era. The price of your life was only £9, that's all they'd give a widow. If she had nowhere to go, she'd have to go to the workhouse.

Later the Harriman men worked at the Port Kembla steelworks. Then, as Joe says:

When the last shot of the war was fired I gave my notice at the steelworks and went with contractors to build houses.

Joe Harriman and his wife had three daughters and three sons, and for the first 20 years his garden was put to use to feed the family.

If you'd seen me in the first 20 years on this block of land you would have seen cabbages and spuds at the front fence, right down the back. You wouldn't see an inch of concrete anywhere. I used to work like a slave and grow all the vegetables to eat on the table: beans, tomatoes, beetroot, spuds, cabbages, everything. I wouldn't have any flowers then, or any of what you are after, the ornaments in the front. All that has been done since the family grew up and got married.

Fame came to Mr Harriman, however, when the garden was put to less practical use. Photographs of his constructions have appeared in

colour magazines and the Wollongong Art Gallery. His front yard folk art is a well-known local attraction of which the Harbour Bridge is the centrepiece.

I did the Harbour Bridge first, the iron frame, when I was a maintenance carpenter in North Wollongong, and I asked the boss could I buy some iron, and the welder and I stayed back one evening and put it together on his bench, see. Then I did all the other approaches and things like that, all just as I know they are, as much as you could build in a small garden. I was working over at the quarry at the time the Bridge was opened and I was at the post office that day when I heard Mr de Groot on horseback had cut the ribbon in front of Jack Lang.

I'd go further than saying the Harbour Bridge was an amazing engineering feat – I know more about the Harbour Bridge than practically any man in Australia, because in 1926 when I was a boy 16, the big coal strike was on, and another three mates and myself went on pushbikes to no end of places, to every

nook and cranny of the county of Durham, and into some parts of Northumberland. And there we saw the foundations of the Newcastle-on-Tyne bridge. They knew then that if they could get this one span of the Newcastle bridge to stand they would have to get the contract for the Sydney Harbour, and they would get that to stand up in one span. The Newcastle bridge is only one-third the size of Sydney Harbour. I knew that as a boy. I never was a bright scholar, but I've got a good memory, like my mother before. You cannot have both things, you can't be a real educated individual, and have a good memory. You are one or the other. I was leaning more towards being a dunce, in the middle of the class, all in public school, but I have a terrific memory.

Using his memory of structure and formation and his experience gained as a builder, Mr Harriman made the Bridge complete with expressways and ramps. The miniature cars are also handmade. The simulated harbour under the Bridge has been adapted to form a goldfish pond. It is constructed of a blue-painted sheet of flat iron with water lilies for decoration.

A controversial feature of Mr Harriman's front garden is the array of greying cockle and cone shells he has used to form the shores of the harbour. While he was building his Bridge, a large Aboriginal midden was to be bulldozed.

The shells – there was a big song and dance about them. They are really historic. They are from an Aboriginal midden. A young neighbour took me for a walk down to Bellambi jetty, and then we walked along the beach a fair way,

The miniature features of Luna Park were all handmade from memory after he made day-trips from the south coast.

until we got to Towradgi. He showed me the Aboriginal midden, where the Aborigines really did eat the fish out of these shells. So a few years ago when the silt was really going, and they were going to build the sewerage plant from the Balgownie hostel, I could see all of this was being bulldozed over, so I got

my pushbike and I went down for a few nights and tried to save some of the shells. I picked them up and put them in a corn bag and carried them back up here. Now there are smart alecs around the place who say oh, I should put them back, they're from an Aborigine's midden. I just tell them it was a great

that greets pedestrians is the children's favourite. The ferris wheel is complete with little swinging seats and another section has what Mr Harriman calls the "crazy place", the old Fun Palace. Mr Harriman feels people should understand why Luna Park is there.

The site of Luna Park was the construction ground to put the Harbour Bridge together. Did you know that? When the pieces of the Harbour Bridge were put together, that's when Luna Park was built. It was only a swampy piece of ground and then of course as the years went by the Ghost Train was burnt out and then they made the Harbourside Amusement Park, but that hasn't been a paying concern.

Mr Harriman clearly derives great satisfaction and pleasure from demonstrating his wholehearted adoption of the wonders of the country he came to when such a young lad.

I think it's a work of art, sculpture, whatever you like to term it. A work of art because nobody has got that in the front of their yard and a lot of people remark to me: "Very, very clever, don't know how you do it, mate." There are no knockers.

As Mr Harriman is now 83, from time to time he thinks of the future, aware that so many other wonderful gardens have fallen into disarray when their makers leave them.

When it's my time to die, I'm going to get a special grandchild of mine, a very brainy boy, to take the place over. I have a good family to look after the place, and my bits and pieces. It would be a shame if anybody just came and knocked the gardens over.

pity they didn't think of that earlier.

After the completion of the Harbour Bridge, inspiration struck again and Mr Harriman commenced his Opera House – a much simpler structure on the side of the front garden. This was followed by Luna Park.

There was a young boy one day looking over the fence, and I had the Harbour Bridge made, and the Opera House, and he says to me "Mister, seeing you've got all them sort of things there, it would be an idea for you to build Luna Park on the other side." So I thought I'd better do that.

Luna Park with its large insignia face

CANBERRA'S LOCAL PARLIAMENT

The cement and steel sculptures of Giacomo Rampone dominate the front yard of the sturdy brick houses he designed in Canberra. Giacomo Rampone builds each of the houses and then sells them.

Born in Italy in 1932, Giacomo emigrated to Australia in 1956, moving to Canberra with his family in 1970. Coming from a very large family, financial restrictions caused him to leave school early so he could not follow his desire to be an architect. In later life, however, Giacomo Rampone has fulfilled his dream: after acquiring the skills and techniques he needed while working as a builder he began to design and build houses.

In front of the first house he built, Rampone offered viewers a replica of the Sydney Opera House. As Canberra's gesture towards its big city neighbour to the north, the Minister for Canberra launched Rampone's sculpture the same day the Queen opened the real Sydney Opera House in 1973.

In 1978 Rampone moved on to design and install a model of Canberra's famous Telecom Tower which stands as a landmark over the city on Black Mountain. Rampone's Tower was not merely decorative, doubling as his letterbox.

The urge to pay homage to the great architectural triumph of the nation's capital, the new Parliament House, came later. Rampone remembers purchasing a postcard in 1989 and from that time, he was moved to devise his current front yard sculpture. This is a formal display of the forecourt of Parliament House, complete with driving ramps to its front doors and the flagpole. The sculpture gives the Rampone house an unmistakably official and formal air.

Rampone's constructions are simplified and minimal versions of the external forms of the buildings he chooses to honour. Paint and tiles are added. Even the presentation, position and landscaping of the garden is formally planned and designed. There is no haphazard placing of objects in Mr Rampone's garden.

It is a relief to see something slightly different in this city of conformity, respectable gardens and neatly planned streets. Giacomo Rampone's originality has brought him notice, and although his former houses have featured in newspaper articles, the new owners of his houses have not been moved to retain his unique sculptures as their own. Consequently only Parliament House survives.

The seat of government moves to the suburbs.

Australia, You're Standing on It

*I*ndustrious folk art gardeners throughout the country declare their pride in Australia with an immense array of national signs and symbols. Most are indigenous cement figurines – kangaroos, emus, wallabies, platypuses, wombats, dingoes, echidnas, magpies, even crocodiles. While some people choose to cover their house with stickers and emblems, or wear appropriate T-shirts with insignia like "Aussies C'mon", numerous Australiana gardeners wave the flag in other ways.

Australian animal fanciers usually paint the surfaces appropriately, although just which species is being depicted is sometimes in question. Magpies metamorphose into currawongs, and it seems koalas can be pink or green. The animals sit on front porches, edge the front garden path or stand proudly against the side fence. Friendly characters, they suggest their owners' fondness for pets with friendly smiles painted on their benign faces. Along with freestanding front yard displays of national icons, like the Sydney Harbour Bridge, the Opera House and Parliament House, gardeners occasionally give the emu and the kangaroo a context in Australia's coat of arms.

Some gardens are ironically planted out with petunias, roses and hibiscus on which the native animals are permitted to graze. Their real ancestors have long since departed the suburban streets in which the cement figurines roam but nevertheless they add an indigenous tone to the garden. Australian maps and leaping kangaroos are occasionally found as decorative elements in walls or gates, perhaps in mosaic work or carved into surfaces, announcing the patriotic affiliations of those within. Upon investigation it is quite common to find that the makers are postwar immigrants, proud of their new homeland and marking this in cement.

Beau Hancock's cut-tin weathervane coat of arms stands in the front yard at Dungog.

THE WELL MAPPED-OUT LAWN

The seaside town of Goolwa, South Australia, is situated at the mouth of the Coorong, that vast lake area formed by the Murray River before it finally reaches the sea. Goolwa is home to many fishing families and has a significant population of retired couples.

Max Kairl's well mapped-out front lawn is his personal patriotic statement.

Most visitors come to quiet Goolwa for seaside recreation, fishing, swimming or perhaps to take the ferry across the mouth of the river to Hindmarsh Island. However, an inordinately large number of buses detour into Brooking Street, although at first glance it seems just the same as other streets in the neighbourhood. The buses stop and disgorge tourists, visitors and school children who come to look over the low timber fence outside No. 1, the residence of Max Kairl.

It is not the small white bungalow with its myriad portable pot-planted flowering shrubs that takes their eye, but the front lawn. It has been carved by hand into a replica of the map of Australia, complete with the states, rivers and special features. The lush bright green map stands out clearly against the bright blue stony sea which surrounds it – like the continent of Australia might look from space if you were just about to land.

Max Kairl is a proud Australian. This is his second personal patriotic statement: he made another Australian map in the front yard of his former house at Fullarton, in the centre of Adelaide. Max has turned his front yard into a living symbol of Australia, the country he loves so much.

For many years in his early life Max

Goolwa is given just importance as the gateway of the Murray River while ships wait at sea to enter Victor Harbour.

Kairl worked as a farmer, then on a sheep station for 15 years, finishing his working life as a builder's labourer. He retired to concentrate on gardening.

Numerous expensive public works were due for completion in 1988 – the year of the Australian Bicentenary. One of these was the historical museum at nearby Signal Point, which according to Max Kairl cost at least $5.5 million. A combination of patriotic fervour and the desire to show what an ordinary person could achieve with little or no cost that could make a similar statement, stimulated Max Kairl to transform his front garden, to map out a new lawn.

I did it in 1988, during the Bicentenary. I had one also in Adelaide at Fullarton. It was the Australian flag and I cemented all around it. Here, I've put the animals and flowers in the different states – black swans for Western Australia, and blue gums for Tasmania. I copied a map I had. First of all I measured out the square in the grass 26 by 18 feet. My map was 25 by 17 inches so I put a peg in the middle of the map, then worked out the pegs for the edge of Australia one inch to the foot, then I chopped the lawn out with an axe around the edge of Australia. I filled in the water with ordinary screenings of half-inch metal, like road metal, and then sprayed it all with blue acrylic paint.

I painted the emblems of each state flower – the Sturt pea is for South Australia, the rabbit and emu in Western Australia, camels, pelican and duck are near Lake Alexandrina, and the river systems I put in as well. The Murray, Darling, Murrumbidgee and Ayers Rock. Ayers Rock has the posts which support the rope for climbers – but I didn't climb up the whole way myself.

I don't know what made me do it. It's a lot of work. I'm 81 years old now. More people should do things like this.

The cardboard signs that mark each state's floral emblem have been handpainted, and are staked to the ground like seed packets. Looking over the fence in the weeks that pass, passers-by might have expected the desert to bloom with Sturt's desert peas and for waratahs to cover New South Wales, but only the packets remain – simply floral insignia.

In the 1950s, tourist maps of Australia characterised each territory by using visual signs and symbols. Max Kairl offers us the crocodile for Queensland, the rabbit for South Australia and the black swan for Western Australia. In the west, the camels of the early Afghans have been let loose, while in the sea around the map (on the blue painted stones) ships await

permission to call in to port, perhaps at Victor Harbour, close to Goolwa.

When the garden was officially opened in 1988, over 200 people gathered for the event. The memory of the day transfixes Max Kairl with pleasure. The garden still attracts a lot of interest from tourists and school children, who come to draw it. He listens from his porch to the teachers explaining various states. A large ladder is kept handy for photographers to enable them to get a better view so that the map looks in correct proportion.

Compared to most gardens, the Map of Australia needs little maintenance; however, Max Kairl trims the edges with shears (a skill he learned on sheep) and mows the lawn once a fortnight. This is somewhat tedious as all the small objects have to be removed. "I take everything off bar Ayers Rock." In addition, each summer the blue paint is renewed on the stone gravel which forms the sea.

During his retirement Mr Kairl has enjoyed travelling around Australia looking at other unusual gardens and he always carries photographs of his garden to show new acquaintances. He is sure he has one of the best and, despite initial uncomprehending glances by neighbours, his garden is now a much loved local talking point.

The neighbours were interested all right when I began the work. I never said what I was doing. I was digging there for days but then when I started to get the model out, the map itself, they woke up to it. Now there's another fellow started something like this a few streets away, with boats and gravel nearby.

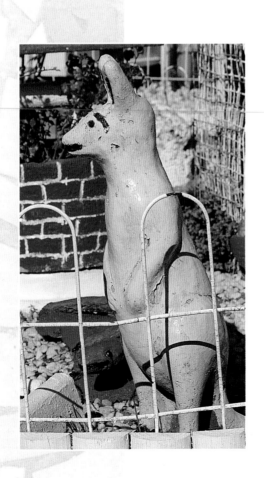

Indigenous Perennials

*Australians show
respect for their
threatened
suburban fauna.*

ACKNOWLEDGEMENTS

Finding and photographing these gardens as well as interviewing their makers took a great deal of time and patience over six years. Many friends became involved and helped in the search. I am particularly grateful to Martin Thomas who journeyed all over New South Wales on my behalf, and to Meredith Aveling, my assistant, who typed interviews, kept the photographic file and also typed the manuscript. Forty-five gardens are represented from 100 or more we visited or considered.

An early influence was the House About Wollongong project, and my thanks to Ruth Waller for her assistance and the use of her photographs.

Local councils in each state responded to my requests for information and staff members may recognise a recommended local garden within these pages.

I am also appreciative of the help provided by *Artlink* after my article "Eccentric Gardens" appeared, and for the impetus this had towards publishing a book. When writing, "Varuna" writers centre in the Blue Mountains provided not only a tranquil space,

heartily good food and company, but also proximity to Cherry Cottage and the Windy Day Windmill Garden.

I am also grateful to the following for help in finding gardens or in other ways: Wendy Barnaby, Jeff Doring, Gail Metcalfe, Maitland and Robin Wheeler, Sylvia Kleinert, Jenny Home, Diane Longley, Garry Smith, Thancoupie, Carole Johnson and Jeanette Davie.

Many photographers came to the rescue, particularly Jon Rhodes, Richard Woldendorp, Ken Stepnell and Irene Lorbergs.

The University of Queensland Press showed great courage and taste in publishing *Quirky Gardens*. My particular thanks to Laurie Muller (who found the Jeparit Junk garden), to editors Sue Abbey and Carol Dettmann, and designers Paul Rendle and the never-daunted, always inventive, Toni Hope-Caten.

My thanks finally to my agent Margaret Connolly for resolutely shepherding the "concept" to the "book".

I wish to thank most the garden owners and makers who cooperated enthusiastically, and my dear husband David and sons Joe, Sam and William for enduring endless detours to strange places with me.

JENNIFER ISAACS

PHOTOGRAPHIC CREDITS
All photographs were taken by the author except for the following:
Dianne Longley: p. 1 (facing), 6, 12, 14/15, 17, 18/19 (with Olga Sankey), 55, 125, 131.
Jon Rhodes: p. 4/5, 37, 84, 86, 88, 89, 90, 91, 112, 144.
Richard Woldendorp: p. 24, 25, 130.
Ken Stepnell: p. 8, 9, 10, 11, 20, 21, 22, 23, 60, 93, 94, 95, 124, 136.
Irene Lorbergs: p. 40, 62/63, 64, 65, 66, 67, 68, 69, 143.
David Humphries: p. 2.
Ruth Waller: p. 39, 58, 101, 138, 152.
Martin Thomas: p. 87, 97, 114, 115, 116, 117.
Brett Hanwright: p. 132, 133, 134.
Peter Evert: p. 80, 81, 82, 83.
Katriona Jackson and Tim Metherall: p. 135.
Tish Banks: p. 148/149.
Australian House and Garden Design: p. 34, 35.